Message of Bhagvad Geeta To The Youth

DR. NALINI V. DAVE

INDIA · SINGAPORE · MALAYSIA

ISBN 979-8-89415-237-0

Dedicated

To
Narendrabhai Modi
Prime Minister of Bharat
A true Karmayogi

CONTENTS

Contents

THE BOOK

Bhagvad Geeta is not related to any religion. It is the book that touches the life of a humanbeing irrespective of race, religion, gender, age or nationality. It addresses the problems faced by the whole mankind all over the world.

This book is not all inclusive. Its focus is mainly on the youth – who is studying or in search of job or working as an executive – building his career. The youth means here all such younger generation living in any corner of the world. Geeta teaches how to live a life with happiness, satisfaction without stress and tension in to day's competitive global scenario. Here the person has to run to stay where he is and it makes life full of stress. Though some level of stress is considered necessary for efficiency, but it must remain at manageable level. Geeta guides in art of living with happiness and harmony in personal as well as professional life.

Therefore this book's focus is on those issues in which Geeta gives useful message to the youth, such as in the areas of motivation, leadership, stress management, managing the mind, attitude towards action (Karma) and the result thereof. Apart from this it also discusses – how the environment protection is possible by contributing into eternal universal YAJGA that is going on by all the natural elements. Other things related to self knowledge (Aatmgyan) is taken only that much which is necessary to understand Geeta's knowledge.

So the book helps the youth to know our age-old thinking, our ethos and values, which guides to live happy and meaningful life.

THE AUTHOR

Dr. NALINI V. DAVE is a retired professor from the Department of Commerce and Business Administration in Saurashtra University, Rajkot (Gujarat). She is M.A., M.Com. And Ph.D. She has taught postgraduate students for more than 25 years. She has also provided guidence to M.Phil. and Ph.D. students.

Her research based studies on topics, like, **"Industrial Sickness and Key Areas of Management in Textile Industry of Gujarat"**, **"Hospital Management"**, **"Vedanta and Management"** etc. Which are published in Book Form are highly significant. She has numerous research papers to her credit published in renowned national level journals. She has received Awards twice from the Institute of Chartered Accountants of India for one of the best Paper Published in its magazine during the year. She has also been honoured twice with the Hari Om Ashram Prerit Shri Bhaikaka Inter-university Smarak Trust Award for the best paper published during the year.

Afterwards **Dr. Dave** chooses to take Voluntary Retirement to pursue the study of Vedanta and dedicated her to this pursult leaving all other activities. She realised that incorporating Vedantic Concepts in Management Practices can enhance productivity, bring meaning to life and lead to greater satisfaction and happiness with less stress and tension for the managers.

Currently she teaches the Bhagvadgeeta and Vivekchudamani to individuals who wish to gain knowledge about Jeeva, Jagat and Ishwer by sharing her audio clips on social media in both English and Gujarati. Upnishads are not reachable to all but Geeta can serve the purpose as Geeta is in Swami Vivekanand's view – the bouquet composel of beautiful flowers of spiritual truths collected from the Upnishads.

This book will be benificial to practising managers, enabling them to be more effective, productive and compassionate in their approach to others within organizations. Their lives also become more satisfying, peaceful and meaningful. Even for the common man, the book may be helpful to understand the message of Geeta.

PREFACE

Bhagvad Geeta is not a book of a particular religion or particular country. It is a universal book which is related to the whole of mankind. It addresses the fundamental problems faced by every individual irrespective of race, religion, caste, gender or nationality. It has universal appeal. Like Arjuna we also face many problems when we feel confused, failed in taking right decision at the right time and also want to run away from the situations. Here. Geeta can guide Us.

Mahatma Gandhi says "When disappointment stares me in the face and all alone I see not one ray of light I go back to the Bhagvad Geeta a verse here and a versa there and I immediately begin to smile in the midst to overwhelming tragedies. Thus, Gandhi whenever feels lost himself he used to approach Geeta and he always finds some solution."

Lokmanya Tilak says. "Geeta was not preached as a pastime for persons tired out after living a worldly life but it gives a lesson that how such worldly life one should live with an eye to be free from the cycle of birth and death. Madan Mohan malaviya says. "Geeta teaches self-control non violence, truth, compassion, obedience to the duty and putting up a fight against unrighteousness" he states further that "To my knowledge there is no book in the whole range of the world's literature so high above all as the Bhagvad Geeta which is a treasure House of Dharma not only for Hindus but for the all mankind."

Adious Huxley says, "The Bhagvad Geeta is perhaps the most systematic spiritual statement of the perennial philosophy."

Thus, Geeta has been relevant for thousands of years and still it is equally relevant and will remain so for all the times to come as it touches fundamental problems faced by mankind all over the world.

There are many Geeta utter Geeta Anu Geeta, Uddhav Geeta, Ashtavakra Geeta but among all Bhagvad Geeta is given much more reverence because here it comes from the mouth of Shree Krushna himself and before him the disciple like Arjuna The original word in Sanskrit is Geetam and not Geeta but here gender change is made as Geeta follows shruti and shruti is feminine word so it is named as Geeta there are also many verses lifted directly from Upanishads and placed in Geeta. Swami Vivekananda states, "The Geeta is a bouquet composed of beautiful flowers of spiritual truths from the Upanishads.

And see the effectiveness of teaching in Bhagvad Geeta by Bhagwan Shree Krushna where Arjuna declares at the end of Geeta, "My confusion has gone, I have gained a clear vision and now no problem in doing what is to be done. This is what that – every human being can say at any corner of the world after studying Geeta when one assimilates its teaching as one's own.

There are many books on Geeta in the market. Every other day someone writes on it. But that book is the most appropriate which upholds the meaning of the words of shastra in the same sense in which these are used and can reach very clearly up to the seekers without creating any doubt in their mind. The first original translation of Geeta in English was published in Bengal by some English men who have learned Geeta from a Bengal Pandit, and then Warren Hastings had given permission to publish it. It was written in its preface that when British Empire goes away then even Geeta will remain.

Adi Shankaracharya has written Bhashya on Geeta. Geeta is not an original text and Bhashya is generally written only in original text. It comes in the middle of the Mahabharata which is an epic belonging to the lunar dynasty (Chandra Vansh). It is historic based on history and very poetic too.

There is no topic which is not discussed in Mahabharata. Rajagopalachari says about Mahabharata that what is not in Mahabharata is nowhere. In Mahabharata there is a main story and within it there are many stories each having some lessen some moral to learn in almost all areas, be it social, political, economic, administration, family relations and what not? Though Mahabharata is a tragedy at the same time it presents dharma and adharma both but the central theme moved around the value that satyam jayati. It gives the message that though ahinsa is the value but if Dharma is threatened, to protect Dharma and to destroy adharma one must fight for Dharma.

So, thus Geeta exist as an Akhyayika. (a story) in the Mahabharata as a Samvad between Bhagwan Shree Krishna and Arjuna but its importance is so high that Shankaracharya wrote Bhashya on it. It contains the most precious knowledge of atman jagat and Ishvar (jeeva jagat and Ishvar) given by Bhagwan Shree Krishna whom Ved Vyas has presented as avatar.

The question may arise in mind why we call Shree Krishna as Bhagwan? There are six bhagas all in total in him so we call him Bhagwan as we say one with a huge amount of wealth Dhanwan, Vidhyawan, Gunwan etc. These six bhagas are all in total.

1. Total Lordship/Samagram Aishwaryam.

2. Total-Wealth/Samagram Wealth.

3. Total Knowledge/Samagarm Janam.

4. Total Dissipation/Samagram Vairagyam.

5. Total Power/Samagram Viryum – Samarthyam to create sustain and to take it back,

6. Total Glory/Sumagram Vibhuti – all talents.

These six fold total limitless qualities/gunas constitute bhagas; Bhagwan Krushna has all the six bhagas in total so we call him Bhagwan.

We human beings also have these bhagas but we have those in limited amounts so we also can say that we are little little bhagwan. Isn't it?

The problem faced by Arjuna in Geeta and the problems we encounter in our daily lives are different but the nature of the problem is the same. At times we also feel sorrow, we may also decide to avoid or escape from our duty. However Shree Krishna advises to all of us through Arjuna – do not run away from your duty, learn to face the situation. This requires inner courage which we find only when mind is calm, strong and balanced this equanimity of mind comes from having a broad vision that recognizes that we are not isolated individuals but rather we are connected and interdependent with the entire universe. When we realize this truth our vision expands into macro vision which is the need of the day for mankind Geeta helps in cultivating such vision.

Dr. Nalini V. Dave

+91 9429880677

FUNDAMENTAL PROBLEMS OF MANKIND

Geeta addresses the fundamental problems of the mankind. Our mind is just like a battlefield where a huge number of desires are fighting to get priority by us. The man is gifted with freewill which no other living beings are given. Animals are programmed but man has a choice. He can select any act to do or not to do or do it in a different way. Along with this man is also given vivek – discrimination power so that on the basis of righteousness he can select his action. Everyone knows what is right and what is wrong. For this one does not need tuition classes. Such Vivek is inbuilt in human being. Even two years old child knows when it lies to its mother that it is wrong.

Another thing that is significant in mankind in general and in particular it is found more in the youth. This is self consciousness and self judgment. Consequently the thinking like "I am not good looking", "I am dark", "I am short", "I am said", "I am unhappy". "Everything is not well with me" etc.prevails. And always you remain busy in removing these notions so far as it is possible. In other words it can be said that you will always busy in the process of "becoming" as you want to feel at home. If you feel sadness you will try to become happy by whatever means available to you. If you are poor you will be busy in becoming rich. For looking more handsome for becoming more beautiful you visit parlour and apply various techniques for that. Thus the whole mankind is busy in this process of "becoming"

Moreover another problem that disturbs the mankind is the sense of inadequacy. You are never satisfied about how you are, what you are, what you have and so always want to have something more to feel up inadequacy and to become happy. Our youth also face the same problem. They feel inadequacy almost in everything. In their look, in their education, in their result in examination, in their job if they have started doing job, their family, other relations, status in the society, economic background and what not? In fact you want happiness always in all places and in all the situations. You want to be satisfied with yourself. For that you try to change the world outside which is mostly not possible. You will also try to earn more, together more wealth, more comforts of life, luxurious bike or car, and many such worldly objects. This all no doubt will provide you satisfaction and joy for some time but again you want to get a few more achievements in your life and you will never get success in getting that happiness which you want as there is no connection in what you want and what you are doing for getting that. You want happiness that remains with you always but you try to get that from the worldly objects which are not nitya/shashwat. They are anitya and so provide you happiness for limited period of time.

Another problem of mankind is that it needs others approval in whatever it does. Thus not only you have judgment for yourself but in whatever you do to change your judgment or whatever you do in the process of becoming you need others approvals too. If by going in beauty parlour you have changed your look you expect others to take its notice and pass some positive good remark. If you have got success in a particular project assigned to you, you need its approval by your seniors, by your colleagues and this makes you feel happy. The fact is all of us try to seek happiness where it is not.

That is why we need "Adhyatma Vidya" which teaches that the things sought for happiness and self approval are already with us. We need only to know that. Here the man has many doubts, confusion and problems. Upanishads can help us as it is doubt resolution knowledge. Swami Vivekananda says that Upanishads may not be in reach of all the people but we have Geeta which is the collection of all beautiful lessons and truths of Upanishads. So study the Geeta and you can find a solution of your every problem.

Most of the problems discussed till now are because you take yourself as body. Body has always many such problems such as "I am unhappy", "I am mortal", "I am ignorant" etc. Thus the mankind feels three major limitations all over the world. These are fundamental problems faced by the universe. These are:

1—Limitations of sorrow

2—Limitations of mortality

3—Limitations of ignorance

Shock, Kal and Ajnan

In relation to these fundamental universal issues bhagwan Shree krushna begins his teaching in the second chapter's 11th versa. He says to Arjuna -you are grieving over that which deserves no grief, although you talk words of wisdom, the wise grieve neither for the living nor for the dead.

In this one versa Bhagwan covers almost all the three limitations faced by the people all over the world.

1. Limitations of sorrow

We all feel sorrow caused by variety of things but basic feeling behind every sorrow is the thinking that "all is not well with me". As man wants nitya happiness he cannot stand sorrow and so tries to get rid of it. Now we know that Geeta is an **AKHYAYIKA (STORY)** of Mahabharata. Arjuna was fully prepared and motivated for fighting adharma and to protect Dharma but when bhagwan shree Krushna brings his chariot in front of the opposite army, Arjuna so his own dear ones. Acharya drona, Bhshma pitamah, krupacharya, his grandfathers his brothers, his friends and many other people. There is a severe confusion in his mind and he deeply feels a conflict between duty and attachment. And then what happens is well known Arjuna feels all the three limitations and experience total helplessness. He saw no solution anywhere.

In fact no one likes sorrow. He seeks happiness always and if sorrow comes he wants to get rid of it as early as possible.

2. Limitations of mortality

Another limitation that men feel is that of time. No one wants to die today. Every person wants to live a day longer this is love for continuation that leads to a desire to have a son or a daughter so that his name remains after his children. Thus no one wants to disappear from this world without leaving a trace. Such a desire is nothing but the desire to be eternal (Nitya) So mortality is limitation with respect to time that also we cannot stand.

3. Limitations of ignorance

The third limitation that mankind suffers is ignorance. If a person does not know to write or to read he or she will at least stand at the window to see what is happening in the street. This shows the inner love for knowledge. People read newspapers magazines and see news on TV to know what is happening in their country, in all other places too. This shows the love for knowledge all over the world. we cannot stand ignorance. We always want to know more and more and so you can see Chandrayaan Mangalyaan and Suryayan etc. The whole life the man remains busy in effort in removing these limitations.

Now think for a moment, will we try to get rid of that what is natural for us? No. For example, if my eyes see clearly will I go to a doctor to complain that "See doctor, do something, my eyesight is perfect". Never. So it is clear what is natural for me I accept joyously.

Bhagwan says that all the three limitations do not exist at all. These are totally illegitimate and so "ashochya" but people try all their life to remove them by various kinds of activities. Any problem can be solved by action only if it is a real one and legitimate. If you see a snake on the road you can choose your action either to avoid or chase it away and it can be solved but if you take rope as a snake in the absence of enough light the illegitimate projected snake and the fear caused by it cannot be removed by throwing a stone or praying to the Ishvar. This issue can be solved only when one comes to know that in fact there was no snake. Thus here the problem is solved by knowledge and not by any action.

Bhagwan also says that as a body no doubt, you face sorrow caused by innumerable factors. You are born so will die one day and your knowledge also remains limited but you are not body, you are "atman" and nature of atman is Anand/happiness. It is sanatan, nitya, never born and so never dies. And it is all knowledge. In second adhyaya of Geeta Bhagwan talks about atman which is SAT – that always exist. Isness is its nature and it is CHITT – that is all knowledge and happiness is its basic nature. Thus atman is called satchitanand.

If isness is Atman's nature then there is no limitation of mortality. As it is all knowledge, no limitations of ignorance and as its very nature is happiness so no limitations of sorrow.

Arjuna's arguments cover all these limitations and he feels sorrow to see all his dear ones in front of him and he thinks, I will kill all of these my people with whom I would have loved to live. A severe conflict he experiences in his mind between his duty and his attachment and he merged into sorrow. He also begins to think either they will be killed by me or I will be killed by them. Thus a fear of death also arises in him and he also says I don't know who will win, thus limitations of ignorance also he feels.

Bhagwan addresses all these limitations in one versa (11th versa of 2nd chapter) and says, Arjuna you grieve over that which deserves no grief or sorrow

One does not complain against what is natural so one never complains against one's being happy. Have you ever complained? No. So happiness must be your nature and whatever is natural is not the issue of complaint. All of you have also experienced that in spite of unfulfillment of your never ending desires you cannot help yourself from becoming happy in certain moments like watching beautiful sunset at the seashore or in the company of school/college friends while cracking jokes, on seeing an innocent smile on your child's face. There you forget everything and be very near to your own self/atman which is Anand Swaroop.You cannot be other than happy person because in fact that you are, that is your nature as the sweetness is the nature as sugar.

So Bhagwan says to Arjuna and all of us too that what you seek does not exist. You want to seek to achieve freedom from the limitations of sorrow, mortality and ignorance as you do not know that these all are already achieved just as the removal of the imagined snake on the rope is already achieved. You need not do anything to remove the snake because it was never there and what exists is only the rope which cannot frighten you

And then Bhagwan begins his teaching and says you are not body you are atman and almost the whole second chapter of Geeta teaches what is atman and who am I? The name of the chapter is Sankhya yoga – the knowledge of atman.

– 2 –

YOU ARE ATMAN – NOT BODY

When Arjuna presents himself as a disciple to Bhagwan Krushna by saying I am your disciple please teach me.

शिष्यस्तेहं शाधि मां त्वां प्रपन्नम्

Bhagawan accepts him as a disciple. Guru Shishya relation begins only when the shishya surrenders him by prostrating unto him and the Guru accepts him as his Shishya.

Bhagwan begins his teaching from the 11ᵗʰ verse of second chapter. He says:

अशोच्यानन्वशोचस्त्वं प्रग्नावादांश्च भाषसे।
गतासूनगतासूंश्च नानुशोचन्ति पण्डिता:॥

You grieve over that which deserves no grief or sorrow, although you talk words of wisdom. The wise grieve neither for the living nor for the dead.

Bhagawan then begins saying about what atman is. But to understand that how I am not body but atman I have to know first about the body.

You know that you have a body, a physical body about which you know everything. But do you know you have not one but three bodies? Sthul shareer sukshma shareer and Karan shareer. Let us see one by one.

1. Physical body – Sthul Shareer

It is made of five mahabhuts-earth, water, fire, air and sky.(Pruthvi, Jal, agni vayu and akash.) It has different parts like legs hands and other important organs like brain, heart, lungs, liver, kidney, etc. which are all intelligently put together for a purpose. In this physical body there are also bones, flesh, blood and other filthy things. All this stuff is so disgusting that if we happen to see them in front of us we cannot even look at them. But this is all so beautifully packed in the attractive package or container that we love it and remain busy in making it more attractive and take a great care of it.This Shareer seems alive but in fact it is insentient/Jad.

2. Subtle body – Sukshma Shareer

Subtle body is made of 19 elements.

Five organs of action—Karmendriya (hands, legs, speech, annus and genetic organs)

Five organs of knowledge—Gnanendriyas. (Ears, eyes, tongue, nose, and skin)

Five prans

Prans are very often misunderstood as breathing in and breathing out but in physiological terminology pran stands for manifested life energy which exercises itself in various physiological functions. Let us see all of them.

1. Pran – Breathing

2. Apan – Extraction – throwing out the mal of Shareer.

3. Saman – Circulation of blood and reaching every essence of input we take to their concerned places in the physical body.

4. Vyan – Digestion of food you take.

5. Udan – Throwing out—vomiting sneezing etc. (At the time of death this pran leaves the body in the last)

Mind, Intellect, Chitt and Ahankar=4

1. Mind – The function of mind is to do sankalp – vikalpa, raising doubts, creating fancies etc. It attracts us towards variety of things.

2. Intellect – In one Upanishad physical Shareer is compared with the chariot/Rath and budhhi as its cheriator/sarthi. Budhhi takes decision on whatever mind has thought. Thus taking decision, giving judgment and coming to the conclusion is the function of intellect.

3. Chitt – Whatever knowledge you have, all are stored in chitt. It works like CPU in a computer. Whenever you want to remember or to get particular piece of knowledge, it will find it out from this storage. This storage house has unlimited space to store every knowledge.

Ahankar/EGO—as a human being all of us have the feeling of I – Ness and my – ness. You always believe that those decisions doubts conclusions etc. are my decisions. I made it. Thus this Aham experience is Ahankar. Technically it is said in Vedanta as ego, which always expresses itself as "I" or "mine." Here full doership can be seen. This is ego.

3. Causal body – Karan Shareer

It is called unmanifested. It consists of three gunas, Sattwa, rajas and tamas in their unmanifested state. Causal body is that level where pure and complete ignorance and total non apprehension prevails.

Thus as we have three bodies physical, subtle and causal, we have also three stages of consciousness waking, dream, and deep sleep when individual withdraws from waking and dream state of consciousness, he is said to be in deep sleep state. Here the experiences of waking and dream state remain in seed form(unmanifested) When he wakes up this became again manifested.

When a man is in deep sleep all the activities of intellect, mind and sense organs are temporarily at rest. This state is known as the state of unmanifested because neither reality nor the world of objects, emotions thoughts are manifest or available for sleeper's cognition.

In short it is the state of known apprehension of reality. The experience of the individual is "I Don't know" complete ignorance is the characteristic of this as there is no intellect, neither reality nor projected objective world. Thus total absence of all kinds of knowledge is the experience of all in deep sleep everywhere.

After having some idea about the body now you have that level of understanding which will help you to know what atman is. Bhagwan says to Arjuna nothing you can stop. Things go on changing every moment. It does not need anyone's permission. Your body also keep on changing but it has no problem of sorrow not even for aging about which you are very conscious as sorrow is always cantered on "I". Body has nothing to do with that. The problem is only that you feel, "I am sad," "I feel sorrow". "I am very thin." The problem is you consider yourself as body and not know Atman.

How you will know about Atman? There are five means of knowledge available to get knowledge of everything in this universe. Without employing the means of knowledge, knowledge is not possible but the means we apply must be appropriate, for example knowing colour of the object, you need to employ eyes here you are the subject, the knower behind your eyes and the colour is the object.

There are five means of knowledge are available to us.

First—Direct perception (प्रत्यक्ष प्रमाण)

These are eyes ears nose tongue and skin. You can have the knowledge of colour, form, shabda smell taste and touch by these.

Second—Indirect perception by inference (अनुमान प्रमाण)

It means direct perception plus inference (knowledge or connection between the two) for example you see smoke then you can assume that there must be fire as you know the connection between fire and smoke.

Third—Arthapatti inference (अर्थापत्ति अनुमान)

Here to get knowledge you have to apply two step assumptions. There is well known example in Vedanta to explain this. Suppose Devdutt is on fast, he does not eat during the day and people know that, but he has not lost weight. So you may conclude that he must be eating in night. This is the two step inference.

Fourth—Upman praman (उपमान प्रमाण)

It is used to explain some unseen object. Suppose you have not seen yak then someone may try to say that it looks like our Buffalo, colour is black but a little difference in form etc.Thus by having example also we gather knowledge.

Fifth—Anupasthiti praman (अनुपलब्धि प्रमाण)

This is where we see absence of object that is seen by applying direct perception. Suppose one has in his hand rose flower. Then he puts it somewhere else, so now you find no flower that was there in his hand before.

With all these means you, the Knower can get knowledge of each and everything. Even scientists also apply these five means to discover new things. Our chandrayaan-3 is also the product of the knowledge that scientists gathered by applying these five means of knowledge.

But none of these means of knowledge can give you the knowledge of your own self/atman you seem helpless. What shall you do now?

All kinds of knowledge are within the five means of knowledge except the knowledge of atman. In Sanskrit 3 technical words are used pramata – the knower Praman – the means of knowledge, and Pramaya-the object of your knowledge. Here you are the pramata,you have five pramans and your pramaya is Atman but you find that atman cannot be seen, smelled listened, touched or tasted. It is not the object that can you know by applying those five means of knowledge and you and I want to know what atman is. Who am I?

Now let us try to know about atman. Generally we take atman as a body and we have age-old notions based on this, like" "I am mortal" I am sad", "I m not good looking" etc.

These five means cannot give knowledge of atman. It is clear that except me/atman everything in this universe is object of my knowledge and I can get its knowledge by applying those five means of knowledge. I am the knower and other things are known to me and these two are always different.

When I see a tree, a building, my car, I know that tree is not me, car is mine but I am not a car, but when I look at my body I see it is me. If my skin colour is fair, I am fair, if my body is fat I am fat. Here did you notice that my body is also an object of my knowledge? I know that my body is fat, I know my body's skin colour, and thus I know everything about my body. Similarly I also know about my mind, my intellect, my sense organs. I know that today my mind is restless. I know the level of my intelligence and I also know about my eyesight, about my ears hearing ability. Everything I know about my physical and subtle body. In causal body there is complete ignorance and neither intelligence nor any other organs are available. Everything is in unmanifested as in deep sleep state but when I wake up in the morning I say, "This night I slept well". Now who is there to say that I slept well while totally your body mind intellect is in the field of ignorance? That is Altman, the knower who knows everything and all other things are its object of knowledge. So you are that knower, the atman and not a body/Sthul Sareer.

All the three sharees are insentient/जड़. In the presence of atman or consciousness they become active and alive. Atman is self effulgent but it needs medium to reflect itself. You know that light can never be seen except through the objects in which it reflects. Similarly atman – or we may call it consciousness – needs medium to reflect. Sukshma/Subtle body is medium through which atman reflects and makes it activate. whoever has subtle body, Atman reflects -from ant to elephant. Table, chair etc have no subtle body or sukshma shareer so these are in sentient.

Such atman is not possible to know by applying five means of knowledge. So we have one more means to knowledge that is saxes means in the form of shabda praman (words of Shastras/Scriptures) Thus Vedas are praman to know the atman Vedas are not manmade they are अपौरेषय. Their mantras are not the product of the mind of man but these are seen by our Arsha Drashta Rishes. As Newton has seen the law of gravitation, he himself has not made it but he discovered what is already there. Similarly these mantras which are there in the creation have been discovered by our Rishes. So as we cannot deny which our eyes see, (as eyes are praman for seeing) we cannot deny what Newton and other scientists say, we cannot deny whatever is said in these mantras. We call it sixth means of knowledge that is shabda praman by applying of which means of knowledge we will come to know who I am.

But the words – shastra's words have their own limitations words can reveal only four things – Jati guna sambandh and kriya. And atman has no jati, it is formless, atman had no guna, it is nirguna, it has no sambandh as it is unattached and it has no kriya as it is akarta. So only literal meanings of words will not help. One needs the guru/teacher, who is well knowledgeable in shastra, who have communication skill to make the essence behind the words (लक्शयार्थ) very clear and Shrotriya who can show that which is conveyed in mantras crystal clear that can be well understood by the disciple.

The Atman Is sat; chitt and Anand our Upanishads say this. Sat means every existence. Atman is all pervasive and isness is its nature, it is Chitt-all knowledge, past, present and future and its nature is happiness. It is the only changeless in this changing universe at every moment. It has no form so no avyava. It is limitless Ananta and one without second. It means everything in this universe exist in all pervasive atman or consciousness.

Thus it accommodates all in itself just like space which is also all pervasive and there is not a single point where space does not exist. (we take space only to understand the atman, in fact space is also an object of my knowledge) Thus as space accommodates all objects in itself similarly atman is also all pervasive and limitless and it also accommodates all things like stars, moon, sun, galaxies, seas, rivers, mountains and all the objects of the world including our bodies. This eternal limitless and Sarvagna atman is in all living beings. But we are limited in everything as a body but as atman we are above any limitation. How? Take an example, suppose there is a pot having capacity of 10 litre space inside. Now the pot is limited by its form which can have only 10 little space inside but space outside in which the pot exists is total limitless space similarly atman is one and all pervasive, limitless, but atman in my body is limited by the boundary of my body so I feel limitations in everything.

Thus atman is self effulgent you need light to see objects in darkness but suppose you are in the dark room and your friend comes and ask "Are you there?"You immediately will reply, "Yes I am here". You will not say that bring me some light so I can see whether I am here or not. So it shows that the knowledge of "I AM " is self effulgent/self-evident but "who am I" is to be known and that is to be known only with the help and teaching of the master.

A question may arise in your mind that how one atman can be in so many living beings? It is simple. You know one sun in the sky reflects its light in each and every object of the whole universe. Sun does not do anything. Only its presence makes possible to run solar plants producing electricity which manifest itself differently depending on its mediums like bulb tube light, fan TV AC fridge and what not? Sun has not done anything. In its presence many things can take place. The sun is not concerned about what happens due to its presence. Similarly our bodies are insentient but in presence of atman they become activated, alive and functioning. Atman does nothing. It is akriya/akarta. Only in its presence our body, mind, intellect work. Here also what we are doing, whether our work is value based or only for self-interest, atman has nothing to do with that.

One more doubt still may arise in your mind that if atman is one, ever present, eternal pure and my atman is the atman in all, then how come a few people are very honest, sincere, committed to their duties and live very simple and pure life but some others are quite opposite and may be criminals also. But here we should remember that the atman reflects through subtle body. The subtle body is always with large amount of accumulated vasanas collected during innumerable past births-good and bad-so the degree to which atman reflects through any subtle body depends on the quality of its vasanas.If the jivatma has not many good deeds to its credit atman does not reflect in its full glory while in jeewatma who has pure vasanas and good deeds in his account atman reflects itself in its full glory. It is just like sunlight. Sun is one and its light is also one. But its reflection in the bucket of dirty water will be vague and distorted while in pure water sunlight will reflect in its fullness.

Now let us turn to the teaching of bhagwan shree krushna in the second chapter, named Sankhya yoga – means the knowledge of atman. Bhagwan says Arjuna that you grieve over that which deserves no grief. Just as the atman in the Shareer has to pass through childhood, youth and old age so too will it assumes another body after death. The wise do not grieve on this. You think that you will kill them but the atman that pervades the whole universe is eternal, isness is its nature. No one can kill or destroy it. Yes their bodies are not eternal. These bodies are born and die. If you don't kill them, then even they are going to die one day is certain. But atman inside their bodies never dies. The eternal existence and isness is its nature. Thus it is nitya which does not die even after the death of the body. At the time of death subtle body leaves the body which has longer life than physical body as it has to exhaust a large amount of accumulated karmafal gathered in its past innumerable births, after completing this birth's prarabdha. Atman has nowhere to go. It just merges into the all pervasive atman outside. Just as the pot of 10 little space capacity when broken the space inside the pot has not to go anywhere. It simply merges with the space outside. The same is true with atman.

So Bhagwan says to Arjuna that physical bodies have an end but the atman is eternal, indestructible in comprehensive, changeless and ancient. (पुरातन) How such atman can be killed by anyone or how it itself can kill others? Atman has no form. As it is all pervasive, it is formless so weapons cannot cut/cleave it, fire cannot burn it, water cannot moister it and wind cannot dry it. O Arjuna, Bhagwan says, know this atman and then there is no cause to be sorrow. In the beginning unmanifested atman manifests with the birth of the body. In between the time of birth and death it remains manifested in the body and on death it again becomes unmanifested. It is natural process and so no cause for sorrow. The DEHI that is atman in all the people's DEHA has no death. So you be only "Nimitt matra", stand up and fight to destroy A – Dharma and to protect Dharma.

Bhagwan gives message through Arjuna to all of today's Arjuna to face the problems and challenges which may come in our life, face them bravely. Never think either to avoid or escape the situation but take the decision and act accordingly which is expected of you in the given situation considering it your duty.

When Arjuna saw his own honourable gurus, elders, friends and relatives on the other side, a conflict arise in his mind between his Niyat karma and affection. He began to think that how can I fight with them, how can I kill them? Similar situation may also arise before you, when you are in same position and you are required to take action against the corrupted person and suppose he happens to be your friend, your brother, your son then you also may face such confusion, but then remember what Bhagwan advises Arjuna. He says-putting aside all your likes and dislikes and affection do only that which is expected in the position you hold. Arjuna was the Yoddha, people respected his capability and accepted him as their leader. And he began to think to live on alms, to become sanyasi and spend the time in search of truth. Now taking sanyas with the goal of self knowledge one needs certain qualifications which is known as sadhan chatushthaya–such as to know the difference between atman and anatman, some dispassion,shamdamadi qualities and desire to be free from the cycle of birth and death. Without passing through karmayoga sanyas is difficult.

So Bhagwan says Arjuna to know you as A-karta atman, not a body. If you understand this and perform action considering it your duty which is expected in a given situation, then such an act will never bind you. So you be a karma Yogi. Be a karma Yogi. Stand up and fight.

KARMAYOGA

Bhagwan Shree Krushna says, Arjuna, I have given you the knowledge of Atman.. This knowledge is not easy, not even so difficult. Knowledge is just to see the thing as it is. If eyesight is perfect, you can definitely see things clearly by opening your eyes. But Atmajnan needs certain qualifications. Person must be prepared to receive the knowledge. Age or any academic qualifications are not important. Only inner structure of certain degree of intellectual capacity is required.

In second chapter Bhagwan says till now I was telling you about Sankhya. (Atmajnan) Now I will talk you about Karma Yoga. In 47th verse of second chapter Bhagwan says:

कर्मण्ये वाधिकारस्ते मा फलेषु कदाचन |
कर्मफलहेतुर्भुमा ते संगोस्त्वकर्मानी ||

You have choice over your action but not over the results at any time. Do not (take yourself) to be the author of the result of the action, neither be attached to inaction

Every human being is born with certain likes and dislikes. **(राग-द्वेष)** Rag – Dwesh are of two kinds – binding and non-binding. Wise men also have likes and dislikes but theirs are not binding. But Rag-Dwesh of most of the people generally has born out of the feeling of the sense of inadequacy. These make men dependent for getting certain objects for which they have Rag at any cost and get rid of those objects for which they have Dwesh. Thus for being happy they depend on worldly objects. Such rag-dwesh makes them busy in various activities. In performing these activities **(कर्म)** they produce karmafal. They have to exhaust (enjoy) such karmafal in this birth or births to come. During the process of exhausting/enjoying karmafal, some new karma also takes place, creating again some new karmafal. This cycle of birth and death goes on and on. How this cycle can be broken? Bhagwan says here that karmayoga can break this cycle.

Bhagwan says in this shloke that work or karma alone is your privilege, never its result. This saying of Shree Krushna has confused many scholars. They interpreted that it says one to perform action without expecting the result. Actually it is not so, because it would mean that He was teaching Arjuna without expecting him to understand? No one performs any action without expecting some result. And nothing is wrong in such expectation. It is natural.

Then what does this 'saying' means? It is very clear that it states that you have a choice in your action, but never in the results. The result is inherent in your action itself and it is determined the moment the action is performed. You can never avoid your karmafal/result of the karma, you performed. One cannot jump out of window and expects the result "falling", not to happen.

So the results of actions are governed by the laws which are not under our control.

These are not man-made laws. These came into existence with the creation itself and so made by Ishvar It is according to His laws you get a particular result, not by your choice. These laws are unknown for us and out of our reach or our understanding. But one thing is very clear that the whole universe is governed by these laws in a much organised manner. So Ishvar is karma falPradata-giver of the result. – Result comes from Him.

You have choice in selecting the action and perform it in this way or that way or even not to do any action. This is your jurisdiction. Of course, you may expect result though you know that result is not in your control. In keeping expectation of result, nothing is wrong. It is natural. It is not a problem at all. The problem lies in your reaction to the result when it comes.

Every result is associated with reaction like feeling of our ego being hurt, self condemnation, disappointment, anger, fear etc. if we don't have expected results. If result is very favourable then it may create greed, arrogance, over ambition etc. Both kinds of reaction do not show maturity.

So what you should do? you perform the action of your choice expecting result, act very carefully so that you can achieve what you expected, plan and execute your work efficiently, then even if result comes totally contrary to your expectations, in spite of all your efforts, do not react. Do not say yourself a "Failure". This is maturity.

Why you are not a failure? Because result comes according to the laws of nature. You are not the maker of these laws that govern the result of your action, you neither know all the laws that come into play in giving you the result, nor you can influence these laws but you know that things are functioning in an organized way maintaining harmony in everything in this universe. The laws that govern the universe are the instruments of the Ishvar who give you the result of your action so accept the Ishvar from whom the result comes. He is karmafalpradata. And remember, your jurisdiction is only to select and perform your work. Result falls in the jurisdiction of Ishvar or laws of nature.

This kind of attitude and understanding works as a shock-absorber. Many executives and students suicide if their action brings contrary result. But if they can see that they are responsible only for what they did. Result is not decided by them. If I did not decide the result, how can I consider myself a 'failure'? This sorrow-absorber attitude can save many precious lives. This happens only by changing attitude to see the things.

There are four possibilities about the result of your action:

(i)   You get expected result

(ii) You get more than expected.

(iii) You get less than expected.

(iv) You get totally contrary or negative result.

Now in first two there is no problem. But so far as remaining two are concerned, you need certain attitudinal change in viewing the facts and in your reaction too. How can this be done?

Two things can change the attitude, Geeta says, one is **Ishvararpan Buddhi** – that is offering your karma to the Ishvar as you offer flower, fruits etc. to the Ishvar. Then what happens? You will be more particular that your action must be pure and right as you are going to offer it to the Ishvar. Now logically if you have offered your karma to the Ishvar, then result will also come from Ishvar. Here attitudinal change takes place. Normally when someone picks a rose flower from garden and gives it to you, you will accept happily, smell it and enjoy its sweet fragrance with thanking the giver. But there is a difference in your response to the same flower, if it is received after having been offered to the Ishvar in the temple by Pujari. Here the gesture is quite different. You will accept with honour, bring it to your eyes and head as now it is very sacred. What has brought this attitudinal change in your reaction?

That is the second thing that brought this change. This is Prasad Buddhi. Here you accept the result of your action which was offered to Ishvar as Prasad from Him. When you accept the result of your action as Prasad, the result remains the same. Vision towards it changes. Bhagwan advises Arjuna that perform the action expected of him and leave the result to the Ishvar. And under the feeling of compassion, attachment, fear etc. never indulge into inaction. Do not run away from the difficult situation (here from battlefield for Arjuna) but face the situation and engage in the right action –

This Ishvararpan and Prasad Buddhi diffuse your Rag-Dwesh. For explaining this Bhagwan gives two definitions of karmayoga. In 50th Verse of Second Adhyaya Bhagwan says –**yoga Karmasu Kaushalam** – Again in 48th Verse he describes karmayoga as **Samatvam Yoga Uchyate.**

Yoga Karmasu Kaushalam means the right choice of karma is yoga. Mere performance of action without offering it to Ishvar and accepting the result coming from Ishvar Himself – as His Prasad it is not karmayoga. Moreover mere "Skill in action" is not karamus Kaushalam as by this criterion even a thief or terrorist could also be called karma yogi. In fact yoga Karmasu Kaushalam means one must choose right action in the given situation by putting aside one's likes and dislikes, one's own interest and that which is Vivek and Value based.

Another definition of yoga is Samatvam yoga Uchyate. Samatvam is not possible in karta or karma. These two are of various kinds. Even in the case of result or karmafal Samatvam is not possible as the result of different kind of actions will naturally be different. Thus "Samatvam" is possible only in the case of attitude towards result. Equanimous Buddhi toward result is Samatvam and that becomes possible only when you consider result as Prasad coming from Ishvar to whom you offered your karma. This attitude can not disturb the mind and with calm mind you will be able to put the things on right track in the case of contrary result also.

So by cultivating this attitude one becomes free from sorrow and no longer contrary result can disturb him. Neither action, nor its result creates any bondage for karma yogi because it is the reaction of the mind to the result of an action that creates bondage. Therefore to be free from the cycle of birth and death one must perform that karma which is expected of him by the situation, offer it to the Ishvar and accept result – whatever it may be – as His Prasad. This attitude will make you karmyogi.

So, Arjuna, be a karma yogi. Do your niyat karma, stand up and fight for protecting Dharma and destroying Adharma.

– 4 –

KARMAYOGA IN PRACTICE

Bhagwan first gives the knowledge of Atman and then also shows a method of neutralising likes and dislikes by cultivating specific attitude towards Karma and Karmafal by living the life of Karmayogi.

Karmayoga is that way of life which is helpful for the youth of the whole universe in making their life more satisfied, stress free and meaningful. Here the attitude towards action and its result works as shock-absorber. In present competitive environment one has to prove oneself at every level for even survival. If one fails in any examination, any test or in any project etc. and if one knows that my job is only up to right selection, good performance and hard effort with full commitment, to decide the result is not my job, it is the job of the laws of nature/Ishvar so how can I be considered failure. Thus, he thinks objectively, and takes the result with equanimous mind which makes him able to find out where things go wrong and correct them too.

We know that our Chandrayan-2 failed at the last moment in Soft Landing on the Moon. But our scientists who have great respect to our Vedic Vision were fully capable to trace out the loopholes they missed to notice and correct them and within three and half years they got the great success in making soft landing of Chandrayan-3 on the South Pole of the Moon and become the first country for landing on that area of the Moon.

But we see the suicidal mentality of the youth in the case of some failure, either in student life or while doing challenging job in executive's life. Here in the absence of the knowledge of Geeta he considers himself responsible for the failure and mentally may collapse leading to certain stress producing diseases. Bhagwan says to view the problem with objectivity. Then you will come to know that for action you are responsible as you did it, but how can you be responsible for the result in which no role of you? Result comes from certain laws which governs the whole universe in a very symmetric way and the same laws decides your result also, and you are not the maker of these laws so never consider yourself a 'failure'. Bhagwan also says never try to run away from the situation by taking drastic step to end your life. Face it bravely and take a lesson from such experience, keep the mind calm and analyse the situation and correct it.

Always remember that every human being has divinity inside with some potentiality. If you get negative result in one place, another door may open for you. If you are in touch of Geeta, you can clearly see that. Take here the example of Swami Vivekananda. See his marks-Sheet in the B.A. examination.

English   -   56

Sanskrut   -   43

History   -   56

Mathematics   -   61

Philosophy   -   45 Total 261 out of 500 marks

Here the students who are disappointed with their grades can get assurance and inspiration from the result of this man who eventually became an incomparable writer and speaker, wonderfully eloquent in both Bengali and English and one of the greatest philosopher of our time. As we can see, there is very little co-relation between university grades and the grades one achieves in great examination that is life itself. The real merits of the person cannot be judged by the result he gets in the education institute. ("The Monk as Man – The unknown Life of Swami Vivekananda – SANKAR)

Bhagwan also gives the message that accepts the fact that the world not creates any problem for you. So, never blame the world, the people, situation, family members, relations, your classmates or colleagues etc. In fact, you are the problem and you are the solution. You, yourself can come out of sorrow by understanding that my problems are caused by my own mind dominated by my strong likes dislikes and main expectations. Thus, Geeta shows the right path in everything that you may face in your life.

Arjuna asked, O, Madhusudan, on one hand you say Karma binds, then why you tell me to do such Cruel Karma? **(Ghor Karma)** Bhagwan replies that it is true that karma binds but it binds only if one's attitude towards action is not right. If you make your every Karma – a Yajna and be a Karmayogi – offering your karma to Ishvar and accept the result as Prasad, it does not bind.

"Na Hi Kashchitxanmapi Jatum Nishthakarmakrut |

A man cannot remain without doing any Karma even for a moment.

So, Bhagwan says to Arjuna, "You may give up the kingdom, you may go to the forest, doing tapas and live on alms (**Bhiksha**) but you can never totally give up doing karma. Even for living on bhiksha you have to procure food, prepare meal. And all organs of your body – external and internal are meant to act only. For any living being total cessation of all activities is not possible. So do the karma expected of you with a change in attitude towards that karma and its result.

In eighth Shloke of the third chapter Bhagwan gives very important message to all of us through Arjuna. He says:

Niyatam Kuru Karm Tvam Karm Jyayo Hyakarmana: Shariryatrapi Cha Te Na Prasidhdhyet Akarman: ||

This saying is very significant for the Youth and the whole mankind. Bhagwan says to do the **(Niyat)** niyat karma because instead of doing nothing, to do some karma is better. Niyat karma means the karma that is expected of you in the given situation. Niyat karma means shastra vihit karma. This concept is unique in our Vedic Culture.

There are many yonies. Only Manushya yoni is given free will to choose the action based on Vivek. In Vedas various kinds of karma to satisfy different desires are discussed. – Like desire for wealth, good job, good family, sons, position, power, even rain and what not? For all these desires to satisfy Vedas also give means like various rituals, performing yajnas, specific kinds of tapas etc. These all are known as kamya karma – means to satisfy our desires to be more happy.

There are five kinds of karma – Nitya karma (to be done daily), Naimitic Karma (to be done on special occasion like birth day, marriage day, shraddh day etc.) kamya karma (to be done for satisfying desires), Nishiddh karma (karma which are prohibited by shastra) and Prayshchit karma (to be done to neutralis our wrong actions).

Nitya and niyat karma is that karma which is done by taking it as duty with no desire to get any result. Our Shastra also does not show any result of the Niyat karma. It is Nishkam karma which makes one a karmayoga.

Therefore everyone should perform his niyat karma without doership and with Ishvarpan and Prasad buddhi. It is the most appropriate and most expected karma. The man has an in built ability to know what is expected of him and what is right and what is wrong. So the one who is Karmayogi will do only that karma which he should do by leaving aside his likes and dislikes. He knows that this karma may be very difficult and risky and he also dislike it, then even he will do it as it is his duty. Such is the spirit of the person who lives the life of karmayoga.

Remember that he has right to choose his action. Though vivekbuddhi is also given for the right selection. But there is the possibility that under pressure of rag-dwesh he may not use vivek and does whatever he likes and ignores his niyat karma. Here Vedas say there is no karmafal for niyat karma but in avoiding, it may create the negative result for the person. So Bhagwan warns us to never avoid our niyat karma. All the Shastra vihit and obligatory karma which are expected as the most appropriate action in the given situation are right actions. Every one either at home or on job should always do the niyat karma sincerely whether he likes it or dislike.

Suppose you ignore or avoid your niyat karma, then what else will you do? Without doing any work human being cannot live even for a moment. So he may become busy in doing other actions which may be illegal, useless or harmful for the doer and for the society also. And remember, inactivity always brings destruction of harmony in your life and cause harm to your family, society and nation too. In the long run it may also result in physical disabilities and intellectual deterioration in you so always do your niyat karma which is expected of you in whatever position you are.

The beautiful concept of karmayoga in Geeta is not restricted to any particular dharma, country or certain age-group people. It is important for all. It plays a significant role to all age group people by providing guidance in almost all areas. It is a dialogue between Bhagwan Shri Krushna and Arjuna. The problems that we face now a days may be different but the nature of the problems and viewing the problems is the same. In a way all of us are Arjunas. We also face conflict between duty/niyat karma and attachment, confusion, doubts and at times may also try to escape from such situation.

Here Arjuna's niyat karma is to fight. Instead of fighting, he faces the conflict between niyat karma, and attachment by seeing his own people on the other side. Then gradually the idea of escapism – running away from the situation takes a hold of his mind. We also face similar situations in our life and have also suffer a conflict between duty and attachment. In such a situation by keeping aside our attachment we should take the right decision. To run away from any problem will never resolve it. Instead we have to face the problem and do our best which is expected of us. That is our niyat karma to perform with Yajna – Bhavna. And this is the real karmayoga in practice.

5

ASSOCIATE KARMA WITH YAGNA BHAVNA

(Yajnarth Karma)

When we listen the word, 'Yajna', we imagine a Yajna Vedi with fire in it and Brahmans are chanting mantras and giving ahuti to the fire in Yajna-Vedi by saying "Swaha", "Swaha". But here in Geeta Bhagwan says your every karma can be Yajna if done with proper attitude.

In ninth Verse of third chapter it is said:

Yagnarthatkarmanonyatra Lokoyam
Karmbandhanah |
Tadartham Karma Kaunteya Muktasangah
Samacharah | | (3-9)

People are bound by action other than those performed for the sake of sacrifice, you do that O Kaunteya; perform action for that (for Yajna) alone, being free from all attachment.

In this Verse it is said, no doubt, actions bound but only those actions bound which are not done for sacrifice – with the feeling of 'Swaha". The word Swaha implies leaving aside the self-interest. Geeta says there are certain actions which never bound.

Which actions never bound? Those which are done with the sense of Swaha/Sacrifice. So Bhagwan says – **'Yajyarth Karma Kuru'** and explains the glory of such actions. Shankracharyaji interprets in his Bhashya on Geeta – **Yajna VAI Vishnuhu** that Yajna is Vishnu. Vishnu means all pervasive. Ishavasya Upanishad says in its first verse:

Ishavasyam Idamsarvam, Yat Kishchat Jagtyam Jagat|
Ten Tyakaten Bhunjita Ma Griddham Kasya Sviddhanam ||

All these –whatever is in this universe is covered or pervaded by the Ishvar. That renounced, enjoy. Covet not anybody's wealth.

The basic sur of yajna is 'Swaha'. The one, who lives one's life with sense of 'Swaha', makes every karma **Yajnarth** means doing karma for Ishvar. For whom this Swaha? It can be for any deity. It is not necessary that you have to perform your karma only for Vishnu. Whoever may be your Ishtadeva – may be Shri Ram, Shri Krushna, Shivji, Hanumanji, Ganeshji or Ma Durga, Laxmi, Amba, Saraswati, offer every karma to that deity. Do it for getting His love or making Him pleased.

So in this Verse it is said that do your karma not for yourself. Do 'Swaha' of your personal interest/sankalp. Do for others. Do it by considering it your duty, your niyat karma. Do not have any attachment and do it as devotion, as a Pooja of your Ishtadeva and makes your every karma, a flower offered to Bhagwan. Such actions do not bind.

Thus **Tadartham Karma Kuru.** Tadartham – for making Him Prasanna. If we don't do karma for Ishvar then we do for our own self. Such karma bounds. Therefore Bhagwan says do karma with yajna Bhavna.

A few people opined that if a man does karma not for his own self or for his own interest and do it for others or even for Ishvar, and then his quality of action may be affected adversely. But remember and note that the word **'Muktasang'** does not mean that you finish your work in whatever way you like. Bhagwan uses another word, **"Samachar"** which also means do your niyat karma, do it with the sense of 'Swaha', do it by giving your best in making it perfect and beautiful. This is Karmayoga.

Thus, this is the message for the youth of the whole universe to learn to work for others, for your Ishtadeva and do it with joy, considering your duty, your niyat karma excellently. There is always a great joy in doing for others, in giving time to the elderly people, by telling a few sweet words of Solace to needy people. And you will see that in making others happy, in bringing smile on the lips of sorrowful persons, how happy you feel yourself inside.

Again in 10th verse of third Adhyaya Bhagwan says:

Sahyajya Prajaha Srushtvapurovach Prahapati |
Anen Prasvishyadhyamesh Vosivashtkamadhukh ||

The Prahapati in the beginning created mankind together with yajna and said, "By this you will prosper, let this be your kamdhenu."

Prajapati (Brahma) says that he created the whole Praja (people) with yajna-bhavna in their mind, means a sense of swaha/sacrifice is in built in mankind. So this is natural. If a man lives his life by keeping the benefits of others by leaving his own personal interest aside is said to be living a natural life. And if his life is based on his own self-interest, it is unnatural. It seems that Bhagwan talks quite opposite than people think at large. People believe that a man will naturally seek first his own interest. Even Goswami Tulsidas says:

"Sur Nar Muni Sabki Yah Riti, Swarath Jani Karai Sab Priti" (Ra.Ma. Ki. Ka-11-2) and we also see that swarth is very natural all around us.

In **Bruhadaaranyak Upanishad** also it is said that no husband loves his wife for wife's sake. No father loves his son for his son's sake. But **Aatmnistu Kamay Sarvam Priym Bhavati |**

People think that they love their wife, son, daughter, father, mother, friend etc. But in reality they love only their own SELF. (Atman) Husband will love his wife till his wife makes his inner SELF pleased. Father loves his son till his son gives him respect. If the son insults the father and harass him, try to take away his whole property will father love him? No. Because the son makes the inner self of the father unhappy, displeased. So accept you love someone because that someone makes your self happy and keep it pleased. So except one's own Atman one does not love anyone in this world as the right place to love is only "Atman as there is no difference between Atman and Parmatman.Both are sat, chit and ananda

It is the way of sanatan dharma that we should not work for our own selves but should work for others – may be for family, for society, country or for Ishvar. Develop the habit to sacrifice your desires, your interest for others.

It is true that this sense of Swaha/Yajna Bhavna is placed in the man by Prajapati with creation itself and such sense of renouncing our interest is in-born quality but we cannot negate the sense of self-interest too. And at the same time we also see this sense of swaha scattered here and there in people also around us. Mr. Bill Gate donated his 90% wealth. He did not do that on someone's advice. The Yajna Bhavna was in him already and it gets awakened and he was inspired to donate. And I am certain that he might have felt more happiness and satisfaction than the happiness he experienced in earning that much wealth – as "Giving" has its own joy than "Acquiring."

Our young generation also may think – that how without self-interest one can work efficiently? But suppose you love someone immensely, will you be not ready to give up even your most favourite thing to make him/her pleased? If you love your grandpa and your parents will you not do what they ask by leaving your own wish? Thus, we do sacrifice always for whom we love, who are our Pujya and respected elders. Thus the sense of swaha/sacrifice is in every one of us. We always let go our individual sankalp for the sake of family. Family will let go its interest for the society and society for the country and so on. In absence of such Yajna Bhavna, no family, no society, no union, no government, army – nothing is possible.

Thus, the sense of Swaha is natural. The purpose behind this is to make our work non-binding. So Bhagwan says – **Tadartham Karm Kuru Kaunteya** – sense of swaha does not say that you allow others to endanger your rights – while having Yajna Bhavna. So Bhagwan says to Arjuna, to fight for the right which is endangered by Adharma and added that you don't fight with your relatives, your Pujneeya but with those who did injustice which is Adharma. Everyone has right to get justice, so fight for the principle of justice without having any Dwesh towards the persons who did injustice to you. This is the attitude of Karmayogi.

See the example of Yudhishthir. He fought against Kauravas and won the war, faught for the principle not out of any personal enmity or dwesh. After victory Dhrutrashtra was living with him and Yudhishthir gave him full respect – daily went in morning and evening to prostrate unto him. On the other hand look at Dhrutrashtra. When the war was over, he expressed his wish to congratulate Bheem by embracing him. He was very strong. By embracing Bheem he wanted to crush him, but Shri Krushna was alert, he understood his intension. So he kept iron statue of Bheem which Dhrutrashtra crushed between his two strong and mighty arms. This was the difference in attitude to fight. One was fighting to get justice and protect dharma and the other was fighting with greed and to maintain power to rule following Adharma.

Next five verses – from 11th to 15th in the third Adhyaya, describe the Yajna that is going on continuously in the universe. If this Yajna continues to function uninterrupted, there arise no problem of polluted environment.

In these five verses it is said to the mankind that you do nourish Devas and in return those Devas also nourish you. In the process both will attain shreyas. Satisfied Devas will give you desired objects, in return you have also to offer a part of which gained to the Devas. Bhagwan says who do not offer the Devas their share are thieves. But those who enjoy the 'remnants' of sacrifice are freed from all sins and added that those who cook food only for their own sake enjoy nothing but sin/papa. Then in next verse it is said, food comes from rain, rain comes from Yajna-Bhavna – sense of sacrifice which comes from Karma. Karma comes from the creator – Brahmaji – and Brahmaji comes from Akshar (imperishable). Therefore the all pervading Brahman ever established in sacrifice – in the sense of "Swaha."

Earlier also Bhagwan has said that by Yajna you will grow– **Prasvishyadhaym.** The growth or Abhyudaya comes if you do Pooja of Devas, make them happy and have their blessings. Bhagwan says it is you to take initiative. Srushti that is created by Prajapati is like that. So if you make Devas happy by your devotion, they will bless you, they will nourish you.

Bhashykar interpreted the word **"Deva"** in the traditional sense like Indra Deva, Varun Deva, Agni Deva etc. and says to do Yajna for these Devas and they will prosper you with wealth, position, praise, even rain – say everything.

But here we also can understand the things differently. Geeta gives solution of any problem if we apply our subtle intellect and never make us disappointed. Remember that Veda also says:

Matrudevo Bhav | Atithi Devo Bhav |
Pitrudevo Bhav | Guru Devo Bhav |

It shows that the word, "Deva" means those who are the alter of our respect, our shraddha, our centre of devotion and pooja. Apart from Mata or Pita, it can also be a tree, the river the mountain, any elderly gentleman. Thus apart from traditional Devas like Sun, Varun, Agni etc. We have Devbuddhi on all those from whom we can get something and for which we need their blessings. We in our Sanatan way of life do stuti of the Moon, the river, clouds, ritus and each and everything of the nature. In Vedas we can see such kind of stutis.

We have seen in karmayoga, no one can have choice over result. It comes from Devas, from Ishwer. When we make our Devas/elders happy by leaving aside our own interest, doing every karma as they wish and to make them happy, they will bless us.

Do not forget that whatever you need, you will get from them. If you are a student, you will get all financial help in your education, all necessary comforts, and opportunity of further study in reputed university here or in other countries – everything these Devas provide you. If you are doing job then your growth in organization hierarchy, your promotion, other benefits and everything you receive from Devas – means your superiors, your boss and persons who are senior to you. So make and keep them happy by your sincerity, honesty, punctuality and by excellent quality of your work. Such understanding and attitude not only brings growth in your overall personality, but it will also be beneficial to your organisation and society too. Bhagwan says Arjuna, that you can do it. Karma done by such attitude does not produce result that binds.

Here a question may be raised that the young people have also their own views and ideas. Why should they always accept the views of elders/Devas to make them happy? Yes. The youth has every right to place its idea and opinion. But here it must be very clear in its mind that – this is my opinion but I will not insist for that as to take decision is the function of Devas. But when Devas see that these youngsters have different way of thinking and there is logic behind it but they are not adamant or insist for the favour about what they think. By seeing such sense of Swaha – sacrificing their own interest – continuously they will be pleased and bless you. So you must trust on their experience and wisdom. They will never harm those who have transformed their every karma – a – "Yajna." They will always give you which are beneficial to you. But they will do all such things only when you make them Prasanna/Happy.

Yagyabhavitta Deva Ishtagbhogandasyante Nah |

Geeta when says something we have to find out the message which may guide us towards right direction.

Moreover we should remember that whenever we get something from these Devas, we have to return a certain amount of it to them back. When they provide you the help you need – **Bhogaha** – now it is your turn to understand that these all are not mine. These all are given to me so you have to reciprocate by giving a part of that back to Devas. You know the Sun's blessings to us. We cannot survive without its presence, so it is our duty to do namashkar in the morning by giving anjali of water by chanting Gayatri Mantra.

If you use and enjoy all things given to you for only your self-interest, you are thief. So as we are indebted to the Sun, Vayu, Agni, Pruthvi and all natural resources and so responsible to use them carefully, similarly we are indebted to our Devas from whom we get our desired objects. So it is our duty to look after them very carefully, lovingly take care of them, respect them and be always helpful and co-operative.

Some people may express their doubt that if we do every karma with Yajna Bhavna and accept result as prasad and feel satisfied then what is the motivating factor behind any karma? What is about our ambition? And without ambition how one can grow or prosper? But here our Shastra gives full consent to have ambition. If you grow and prosper, be wealthy, the whole society and your country also be benefited. But remember that the means you apply in fulfilling your ambition must be fair and value based. There is nothing wrong in having ambition and earn more money but use always righteous means to get it. If you have wealth, you can undertake various social activities to help the needy people. If you enjoy your wealth not alone but share it with others, then there is nothing wrong.

We in our culture respect wealth. It is Lakxmi, wife of Vishnu. Rishies call her Devi. Without Lakxmi no dharma karya or charitable acts are possible. So ambition of being wealthy is nice but after becoming rich if one does not share a part of it for the society, one gathers Papa. But if one enjoys **Yagyashesh,** one becomes free from all Papas.

Thus, you can make your every karma a Yajna by having the change in attitude to view the karma and karmafal. Leave all your rag-Dwesh, give your best and make your karma – **Yajnarth.**

6

NITYA YAJNA IN THE UNIVERSE

Geeta describes the continuous Yajna that is going on in the universe in third Adhyaya. It says the 'Sam' Swar of the music – sense of 'swaha' – brings all sweetness very beautifully. Bhagwan shows it in three shlokes of this Adhyaya (14-15-16). We may call it **Srushti Chakra/ Yajna.** Here the whole universe moves in one sur and one Tal with unbroken harmony.

Bhagwan says in these three verses that all living beings come from food. Food helps mankind to survive. The food is produced by rain, rain comes from Yajna, yajna is a product of karma, and karma comes from vedas which are not manmade but came into existence with the creation, just like all laws of science. We know that scientists discovered these laws, not made them. Similarly Veda's mantras are discovered by our Arsha Drashta Rishis.

Vedas cover almost all the areas – consequently any karma done by ordinary farmer in the remote village, happens to do that Vihit karma given in Vedas. These vedas come from Akshar. Here AKSHAR means Ishwer. So eternal manifestation of Vedas is established in Yajna. This all that is said in those three Shlokes.

If you have the sense of swaha and feel happiness in doing well to others, you are a mature person. In fact every one of us must have experienced sometimes in our life such a joy when we have brought smile on the lips of persons by helping them in times of need by money, or by speaking sweet words or by giving solace or merely listened their pain or their problem.

Bhagwan uses the word, 'yajna' in Geeta frequently. He also describes twelve kinds of yajnas in fourth Adhyaya. So it is clear that yajna does not mean only that yajna where ahuti of dhanya or dravya is given to the fire in the yajnavedi. But every karma you can make a yajna with change in attitude.

Yajna cannot be done alone successfully. It needs contribution and co-ordination of all. People should learn to leave aside their personal interest, their rag-dwesh, their individual differences and do not insist that what 1 opined, must be accepted and be always ready to share with others whatever gains are achieved. We see now a day's our Prime Minister, Narendra Modi is doing such yajna by giving ahuti of his personal interest, his time, energy, skill – everything by following the Mantra of **"Sab Ka Sath, Sab Ka Vikas."** Thus, a great yajna, this man alone has begun against all kinds of obstacles for the Rashtra, expecting our ahuti too in the form of full co-operation and the best performance, wherever we are. It is now our duty to stand firmly with him.

In traditional sense Geeta has explained in those three verses that what yajna is, how one comes from the other and how all of them keep the yajna continue by helping one another.

Now let us view the whole process in context of present scenario. Let us take 'Parjanya' – rain – as favourable or conducive atmosphere. When we work for others, with the sense of "Swaha" – sacrifice – conducive atmosphere will automatically prevail. It always helps in getting success in whatever we do, so rain is nothing but favourable atmosphere. And success that it brings is food and other consumer objects. Which maker people's life more comfortable and happy. Such people are more productive in farms and factories.

Thus, yajna Bhavna behind every karma is here very beautifully described in the srushti chakra or the Nitya Yajna that is going on in the whole universe. This great yajna brings Parjanya (conducive environment). Conducive environment brings more production in every sector. But this all become possible only if all involved in this great Srushti Yajna have the sense of swaha and give ahuti when it turn comes.

This yajna goes on and on without any break as all natural forces give their ahuti regularly. The Sun gives its ahuti of its heat by its rays. By leaving heatness Sun plays its role in the yajna. These rays of heat fall on water ponds, lakes, oceans etc. Those all accept the Sun's ahuti and in return they give their ahuti by letting its water transfer into Vapour and help in forming clouds. Vayu in its turn helps clouds to take them where they have to reach. Now clouds also give ahuti in the form of rain to the earth. Earth in turn gives its own ahuti by producing food, keeping forests green and makes the earth beautiful, up to this the process of the universal yajna goes on smoothly. But in the last stage whatever the earth gives to the mankind, there the process is likely to be disturbed.

We know that Prajapati has placed the sense of sacrifice/swaha in the mind of the mankind. All the five Mahabhuts, of which this jagat is made, perform their role magnificently in this **"Pravartitam Chakram"** or universal yajna. Other living beings are also contributing as they are programmed. Only problem is in the case of MAN.

The natural forces never break the Sur of harmony of this yajna. Only the Man who is given a choice or free will may creates a problem, as he can select what to do or not to do or do it in a different way. No doubt, Ishwer has also given him vivek buddhi (discriminative ability). But he is free to ignore it... and do whatever he likes under the pressure of his rag-dwesh. He may not give his ahuti when his turn comes. Instead he may cause harm to the earth, to the water and the air and now we witness of his wrong doings and its serious consequences all over the world –

We have seen from the Sun the process of this yajna chakra begins. Then water, Vayu, earth and all other living beings give their ahuti. Thus Sun leaves its heat; water leaves its form and let it turn into vapour – forming clouds. Clouds leave their water in turn and give ahuti to earth by raining. Earth also in return gives the mankind the food to nourish them and here when the man does not return its ahuti, the Sur and Tal of the yajna that is continuously going on in the universe breaks.

Bhagwan says that the universe can prosper as a whole only if everyone does one's Niyat Karma by considering one's duty with yajna Bhavna. The prosperity is possible only by sacrificing self-cantered narrow interest and by thinking and acting on bigger canvas. Such sense is natural in other yonis but the man has to cultivate such sense of sacrificing his own personal interest consciously.

In Bhashya Bhagwan Bhashykar raises a question; does it mean that Geeta gives the message of only karma with sense of 'Swaha'? What is about those who have no interest in karma and whose only goal of life is to gain SELF knowledge? Bhashykar himself gives its answer too. He says for those whose only goal is Moksh, have no karma to perform. They are made free from all obligatory duties and society takes responsibility to provide them basic necessities of life. But for other people it is not so. Geeta's message tells the people that karma is no doubt binding but with the change in attitude it can be the means to get Moksh. If a thorn went deep into our foot, we need the other thorn to get it out, but after removing the thorn from our foot both thorns we throw away. Similarly Shankracharyaji says karma is the means and Moksh is the end. By passing through karmayoga and by making every karma a 'yajna' one becomes qualified and worthy to gain knowledge (Atma-Gnan). But till then karma is necessary and it is to be done with yajna-bhavna.

Now-a-days we don't see such vision of sacrifice in people at large. They destroy forests. Even on the slops of mountains they build houses and hotels etc. People pollute water by letting go dirty water into rivers. They dump industrial waste in oceans and other water ponds. They also throw poisonous gas into the air. They also took out by digging the earth everything it has in its bosom. Due to such misbehave with the nature we see floods, polluted water, and air. Landslides in mountain areas, earthquake and many such nature's calamities occur due to the irresponsible and self-cantered actions of the mankind.

Now it is the responsibility of the young generation to enlighten the people to think on bigger perspective and have a macro vision and stop to harm the nature. Without natural resources man's living is not possible. The man needs pure water, pure air, fruitful earth, light and heat of the Sun and what not? We are indebted to all of them. Without them we cannot survive. So we should take care of all of them and then only they will provide us what we need for our healthy life.

7

SWA-DHARMA

In the case of the word 'Dharma', we see confusion in its interpretation. This word, 'Dharma' in Sanskrit is the most elusive word for translation in English. It is used mostly in more than one context. Terms like righteousness, good conduct, duty, and noble quality are some of them. Dharma is not to be taken as people say – Christian Dharma, Islam Dharma, and Baudh Dharma etc. In simple way we can say that dharma is to do the most appropriate and niyat karma. Man is given free will and along with it vivek also is given. So everyone knows what is right and what is wrong. If I do not want to get hurt by others, so I should also not hurt others. This common sense is given to everyone.

Sanatan defines Dharma as **"Veda Pratipadit Prayojanayan Karma–** means that karma which is accepted in Vedas as 'VIHIT KARMA" and which has some purpose.

Dharma falls into two categories –

(i) General laws – Samanya Dharma – Universal (applicable to all)

(ii) Specific laws – Vishesh Dharma – Depends on the Status of a person.

Satyam Vad – Dharmam Char,
Chori Na Kuryat – Hinsa Na Kuryat

Such laws/dharma are universal and so applicable to all the people in every corner of the world. But the youth should note that dharma can never be absolute. It is relative. Before exercising any duty or Karma you have to use your intellect, your Vivek Buddhi and then decide to act or not to act. For example it is dharma to say the truth but if some man runs after the cow to kill her and asks the person sitting in the way to which direction that cow is gone. And if that person shows the wrong direction, he tells lie, no doubt but in the given situation his dharma is to save the cow. So in the application of dharma 'Vivek-Vichar' plays an important role.

This Samanya dharma is not man-made. They came into existence with the creation itself; therefore they are not separate from the creator of these laws. We may say here that Ishwer Himself manifests as dharma.

Second category of dharma is of specific nature – Vishesh Dharma – These apply to those who are in Particular Position, Varna, Status or Asharam. They apply to only certain kind of people. For example, dharma of husband, dharma of wife, son, daughter, employer, employee or any ashramist. Here one's dharma cannot be followed by others.

Moreover our universal or Samanya dharma is not mandatory. In Christian religion and in Islam religion dharma mandates are given by the God. It seems here that God says that if you don't follow my mandates, when you come here, I will see you. Their God seems Vindictive. While in our Vedic Vision has no such attitude. Here man is given free will to choose what to do and vivek also on the basis of which, action he may select. And then leave him on his own. It is assumed rightly that people know all "Dos" and "Don'ts" as dharma is known to all.

And it will definitely your experience that whenever you do right thing at right time, you feel joy and satisfaction inside. As in Vedic vision dharma or general laws are not man-made but came into existence with creation and so in our View Ishwer is not other than dharma. In fact dharma is nothing but the manifestation of Ishwer. If I decide to follow the dharma-means that karma which is expected of me – in the given situation. I will do whether I like it or dislike. I will not allow my rag-dwesh to control my decision. Here I don't follow any mandate but I do that considering it my duty and to have peace in my mind. And I will enjoy doing right thing which will help me to grow inside.

Bhagwan says in 35th Verse of third Adhyaya about one's dharma.

Shreyan Swadharmo Vigunah
Pardharmatsvanushtitat |
Swadharme Nidhanam Shreyah Pardharmo
Bhayavah | |

Better one's own 'duty' though devoid of merit, than the "duty" of another well-discharged. Better is death in one's own 'duty', the duty of another is fraught with fear.

Here what is swa-dharma? Whatever is proper as par my age, nature, Varna, ashram, position and status, is my duty or swa-dharma? Swami Subodhanandji explains that swa-dharma is three stariya – (of three levels). First is our swa-dharma from social view point – suppose a person is in certain position – say, collector, judge etc. He has certain duties or dharma to perform in that position but this kind of swa-dharma is for a limited period of time. After retirement that does not remain his swa-dharma. The second is from the viewpoint of our shastra. In whatever role the person is he has to follow certain duties or dharma and this is for the whole life like what is required of his role-whatever it may be (husband, father, son, Guru, Shishya) and whatever is expected of him in any situation he may have to face in his whole life. And the third is what you are in your view. Bhagwan wants to say that when you see that this karma though is your swa-dharma, you feel it very difficult, challenging and problematic, then even if you follow your dharma, do your niyat karma and avoid to follow others' dharma and if you do that, then in your eyes you will rise as a brave and mature person. Therefore do always what is your dharma and never follow others' dharma.

Here it seems that Bhagwan talks contrary to the popular thinking of people at large. Generally people believe that one should do that karma in which one feels comfortable and have interest. So according to one's aptitude and interest one should select one's karma. Bhagwan says, "NO." He says, it is possible that your swa-karma may be difficult, problematic, risky and demands your sacrifice of many things you like and you may think others' karma is better for you and you can perform that work with more proficiency, then even following swa-dharma is beneficial and **(Shreyaskar)** for you and to follow others' dharma may be harmful not only for you but for the whole society. So comfortability and proficiency in performing any work is not the standard to select your dharma/karma. So you have to apply your vivek buddhi and should do self-introspection and then decide your swa-dharma.

When Arjuna told Bhagwan Shri Krushna that he will spend his life on alms and take Sanyas instead of doing this Ghor (Cruel) karma, his focus was not on his interest or proficiency in performing work but he was disturbed by seeing the cruelty in his karma and conflict that he feels in his mind about duty and attachment. In this state of mind he considered to live as a Sanyasi is more ruchikar/interesting and easy. He came there fully motivated to fight but by seeing his own people on the other side his aptitude totally changed. But his swa-dharma was to fight, and not to follow others' – sanyasi dharma – therefore Bhagwan says:

Swadharme Nidhanam Shreyah Pardharmo Bhayavah: |

Bhagwan also says **Shreyan Swadharmo Vigunah** so stick to your swadharma only.

Now here a question may arise in the mind of the youth that, on one hand it is said Vedas are Praman. They describe only about Vihit karma which are always expected to be done by the mankind and on the other hand here it is said that even if Ved Vihit Karma is 'Vigun' then even it is your swadharma to do that only. Now how can be the Ved-Vihit Karma can be "Vigun"?

Yes, it is true. Ved-Prerit and Vihit karma can never be 'Vigun'. But an individual takes it wrongly as 'Vigun', as it seems to him very difficult, risky, problematic and causing him a great financial or other kind of loss and demanding a great sacrifice of his time and strength. Sometimes he thinks, it may affect his social relations adversely so he avoided performing his swadharma and following others' dharma.

If I am Kshatriya by gunas and instead of the karma of Kshatriya, I consider Vaishya's dharma more interesting and profitable and began to perform its dharma by leaving my swa-dharma, then it is harmful in the sense that due to my various good qualities earned in my past births, it is my duty to strengthen these qualities in me. It is my swadharma and not that I open a new area for me and accumulate new Vasanas and continue to move in Sansar-Chakra and lost all whatever I have earned till now in my innumerable births and also lost an opportunity to develop my qualities and moving in the higher level – reaching the level of Sattwa Pradhan.

Moreover in any case we should always be swadharma parayan and not ruchiparayan. Keep in your mind the example of Hanumanji. He had so much strength that he can destroy the whole Lanka and bring back Sitaji too, by killing Ravan and his whole army. But it was his swadharma to do only that much as Shri Ram has told him to do. Hanumanji should do the karma/job assigned to him not according to his strength or interest or aptitude but does that which is his swadharma. What is his Swadharma? It is to do that which Bhagwan Shri Ram wanted him to do. So Hanumanji's swadharma is restricted only to bring news of Sitaji and come back. So keep your life style swadharma Parayan and not Ruchi Parayan. So exercise only your Swadharma and not others' dharma.

From spiritual viewpoint Par-Dharma or others' dharma means to have "Jeeva Bhav" – **(Jivatva)** means to consider one's self as body which is dangerous **(Bhayavah)**. And to end this jeeva bhav and establish oneself into Atma Bhav **(Atmabhav)** is swadharma. What a beautiful way of Presentation? But here let us not go deep into this matter.

In practice you only remember to do that karma which is your niyat karma, what is expected of you in the given situation. Do that karma irrespective of any other thing – Like whether you like or dislike it. Whether it will prove very difficult causing you harm economically, socially or in any other way. Do that as it is your swadharma – by remembering **Swadharmenidhanam Shrey Pardharma Bhayavah: |**

8

INDIAN ETHOS IN MANAGEMENT

When the youth joins either in any organisation as an executive/manager or starts his/her own business, he must have the knowledge of Indian Ethos which helped our civilization to survive since thousands of years against all the obstacles.

Apart from this he/she should also know the vision given in Geeta about leadership, motivation etc.

Here we begin with Indian Ethos – Oxford English dictionary defines Ethos as "The characteristic spirit and beliefs of community/people "which distinguishes the one culture from the other' Indian ethoses are drawn from the vedas, the Ramayana, Mahabharata, Bhagvadgeeta and Upanishads. We Indians are used to manage our trade and industry according to this ethos.Management was not something new to Indians. The MAHABHARAT (Shanti purva) and Kautilya's Arthshastra discussed the management of the state in detail. Our spiritual leaders were great organizers. Indian managers should remember this rich heritage and base their role as a manager on Indian ethos. Some of these ethoses are discussed here.

1 Vedantic View of KARMA
(Transfer of Organization's Members into Karma Yogies)

KARMA or work is considered as a duty and means for individual development and growth. It is very natural as only dead-body is non-working.

Moreover Indian philosophy teaches to perform every work without having any attachment to result, because results do not fall under the jurisdiction of a doer. These are under the jurisdiction of the laws of nature. Hence, one should understand that every action produces result and it is inherent in the action itself and is governed by the laws of nature and one does not know all the laws which contribute to the results but one does know that THINGS function very systematically and in an organised manner in this universe according to these laws. Even the floods, famines, earthquakes occur according to these laws. You are free to act/work or not to work or how to work. It is your jurisdiction. But the result is not under your jurisdiction.

Today we are living in the changing environment with full of problems and threats on one hand and opportunities on the other. A question may arise – how can we turn managers into karma yogis? But it is possible. Lord Krishna has turned Arjuna into a karmayogi in the battlefield itself. Mahatma Gandhi has also turned the Indian people into Karmayogis during freedom movement. A large number of youths have dedicated their lives to the cause of freedom without thinking about the results. Thus, manager's managerial skill lies in his ability to transfer his team-members into Karmayogis. This is the great message given by Geeta for managers. Swami Vivekananda also states that work for **"ATMANO MOKSHARTHAM JAGATHITAYA CHA"** that indicates to gain perfection in individual life as well as for the welfare of others. Thus, the concept of social responsibility has also its roots in Indian Philosophy.

2 Welfare of All –(YAJNA SPIRIT)

Management in developed countries emphasise on profit and productivity. Its major goal is to obtain material success and major share in market. Moral and ethical values have no place in business. Even P. F. Drucker has rejected the idea that business can run on ethics in 1985.

In Indian Philosophy also material success, profit and large market share no doubt are considered important but PROFIT is not the only goal in business. Vedanta teaches to perform all the activities **"ATMANO MOKSHARTH JAGAT HITAY CHA."** Serve your personal interest but do not forget others. Shankaracharya has given the concepts of "NIH SHREYAS and ABHYUDAYA" which preaches to gain perfection in individual life as well as the welfare of the whole world.

In western world also a change took place since 1988. Kenneth Blanchard and Vincent Peale wrote a book "The Power of Ethical Management" (William Marrow and Camp, New York). On the cover of this book was written the line, "Integrity pays, you don't have to cheat to win". At another place a sub-title was found, "Managing only for profit is like playing tennis with your eye on the score board and not on the ball."

In Japan also business ethics have been developed. ZEN teaching accepts all work as a kind of meditation. Thus, Japanese people were inspired more by the spiritual motive for doing well to their nation and the world. The Matsushita Electric Company has taken a leadership in this direction and it has established Matsushita spiritual values for its employees.

In India such thinking was there from the Vedic age. GEETA is the bouquet of Upanishads. Lord says in GEETA, Chapter – 3, Stanza 13 that all the sorrows from the society would be removed if socially conscious members of a community feel satisfaction in enjoying the 'Remnants' of their work performed in the 'YAJNA SPIRIT". He added, "Those who cook for themselves are criminals". What an enlightened idea expressed thousands years before!

A lesson is given in Indian philosophy, "Do your work considering it your duty, earn according to your ability but spend a part of your earning for the welfare of others". Thus, business enterprise is to be based on the concept of YAJNA SPIRIT (Sacrificing individual desire in favour of larger benefits of others). Gandhiji's trusteeship principle has also been emerged from this basic concept. The chapter on KAPIL-DEVHUTI-SAMVAD in BHAGVATAM also describes more clearly the concept of social responsibility. Thus, the concept of social responsibility reflected here in a unique Indian way.

Moreover in Geeta it is said that the universe is an undivided whole, where every particle is connected with every other particle. Lord Krishna says to Arjuna, "I have interpenetrated this universe like pearls on string". This is the Indian vision, which is holistic vision where each one is basically connected with others. Hence doing well for others ultimately does good to the doer also.

Today science has also shifted from the Newtonian I-THOU fragmented dualistic world-view to this holistic world view emerging out of Heisenberg's uncertainty principle, the latest discoveries in Quantum Physics and the successful experimentations of Bell's Theorem. This has much similarity in our holistic vision of Vedanta philosophy.

3 Unique Work Culture

Work is considered as duty or SADHNA. And there is no difference between Karma (Work) and Dharma (Religion). The term 'Dharma' does not indicate any particular religion. DHARMA is a DUTY to be performed in a given situation. Thus Dharma is possible through Karma only.

Purpose of work is growth and development. Work is very natural and only means available to a man for further growth. Work or action results in experience – favourable or unfavourable which slowly enriches one's life. Living human being cannot remain but working at physical or mental level. Through work only one can bring out the divinity and reach the higher stage in this life and the voyage of lives to come.

Moreover in Indian philosophy each and every work is considered equally important. No work is either superior or inferior. What is important is attitude behind the work. Even sweeping can be performed with love and interest which makes it important. Every work is sacred. Hence, a leader or manager should consider every work as important as all other works, accepts the dignity of labour, and should not create any complex in the mind of others during his behaviour with them.

It seems that we have forgotten all these invaluable messages during the British Rule. Now the need of today is to recall all these values and incorporate them in our daily life. Our youth should take its responsibility. These spiritual and philosophical ideas of Indian Ethos have been put to extensive practical demonstrations by some of the Indian companies like, Indian Oil, Air India, Gujarat Ambuja Cement Ltd., Tata group's companies, etc. which are acting as eye openers for many.

In the second chapter of GEETA, Lord Krishna has defined YOGA (Stanza 50 & 48). He says, "YOGA is dexterity/skill in action" and "Evenness of mind/"

Hence "Act established in equanimity, abandoning attachment". Forget everything except the work you perform. In that case you will not care for the success or failure – you will just engross in your work only.

Suppose, in spite of this you do not get success. Then what should you do as a manager? You should accept the result with calmness of mind, showing emotional maturity. This equanimity of mind will provide you a capability to face even the worst situation. Equanimity of mind makes possible a deeper introspection and will enable you to see clearly where the things went wrong and why?

4 Means Are Equally Important as the Ends

Means are given equal importance in our culture. Objectives of any organisations must not only be in correspondence to the values prevailing in the society but these must also be for the benefit and welfare of all – individuals, organisations and society. Means applied for achieving the objectives must also be pure, just, honest and non-harming.

We find around us much dishonesty and corruption and we also find such people wealthy and happy. This creates doubt in mind of the youth about these values. But one always has to pay the cost for the things one gets. Such people do not have any mental peace or happiness within. They suffer from several stresses generated diseases. They live their life in midst of various kinds of fear and threats.

In fact nobody likes dishonesty, corruption or falsehood. Even the greatest of the liars does not want someone else to lie to him. Even a man, who hurts others, does not want himself to be hurt. Thus, dishonest and corrupt people also expect honesty from others. Similarly, everyone loves kindness, honesty and to be loved. Don't you like if someone serves you with love and kindness? This indicates that we have values for all these things in the core of our hearts. These things are our nature. Hence, purity in means is emphasised.

5 Managing Human Resources

Management of human resources is an evolving science. Any business is considered as sound as its people. And management of people is not that easy. A large number of theories and concepts have been developed in western management philosophy in this area. We also do have some principles to guide us from the Vedic age.

Our RIGVEDA offers a comprehensive vision of corporate life in the following MANTRAS:

Common be our Prayers

Common be our Ends

Common be our Purpose

Common be our Deliberations

Common be our Desires

United be our Hearts

United be our Intentions

Perfect be the union amongst us.

Today we are thinking about 'PRAYERS' in the morning,(Japanese management) management by objectives, involving people in determining objectives, taking interest in their personal life etc. All these elements with some other valuable concepts we do have from the Vedic age. If the above MANTRAS are followed in organisations, problems can be minimised and productivity can be maximised.

OM SAHA NA VAVATU

SAHNAU BHUNAKTU

SAHAVIRYAM KARVAVAHAI

TEJASWINA VADHITAMASTU

MA VIDVISHAVAHAI

OM SHANTI, SHANTI, SHANTIHI

Om, May the Almighty protect us both (the preceptor and the disciple, the manager and the subordinate) May He nourish us both. May we work together with great energy, May study be vigorous and fruitful. (Keeping pace with advancing knowledge in respective areas). May we not hate/quarrel with each other. OM, peace, peace, peace.

Apart from this every activity including business is based on concepts – given in our scriptures – like YAJNA SPIRIT which implies sacrificing individual desire/interest in favour of larger benefits of others, (SREYAS), which implies preferring long-term benefits over short-term gains and SHARING, which implies sharing of prosperity, earning and everything with others, where business is viewed not as a means of profit-making but for the overall development and growth (Physical and spiritual) of individuals, and organisations and the whole mankind towards its perfection.

6 Macro Vision

Most of us suffer from micro vision and self-centred views of life and face so many problems and conflicts. Instead of this we are required to develop macro vision as taught in our Vedanta. We should try to understand and accept that I am not a single solitary individual but I am a part of the whole universe. And this universe is nothing but the manifestation of the Ishvar in different forms and names. And all of us are interrelated with each other and every one of us has certain role to play, certain responsibilities to exercise towards society. Such understanding develops a macro vision in us.

Developing such macro vision is the need of today's world.

Globalisation has made the world a 'Small village'. All the nations have now woven into one fabric. An event that takes place in one place can affect the whole world. Hence, management has to learn to view the situations on bigger canvas by coming out of its micro vision, and keeping in view the welfare of the whole mankind while taking any managerial decision.

Our Vedanta has such macro vision due to which our Indian Culture and Civilisation have survived and remained as precious as ever. Now great thinkers of the western world including some of the great scientists have also started to accept the oneness of the whole universe.

Thus, this Indian Ethos has strength to turn the whole scenario inside-out.

But here a question may arise in a mind of the youth that inspite of having such valuable concepts with us since centuries together why we see all around decline and fall of these values and corruption, dishonesty, insincerity, laziness, etc. A nation which has a very rich heritage of culture and values and which has drawn the attention of other countries in the early times and even today, why it itself suffers from so many problems?

This may be due to the wrong interpretation of the values and concepts of our Indian culture by some vested interests – like determination of caste by birth, [In fact, our scriptures state that a caste depends on GUNAS/Qualities – inborn and acquired and karma] blind and mindless pursuit of rituals etc. These vested interests wanted to have all power in their hands by denying education and access to knowledge etc. to majority of people. Women, traders and workers became their victims. Manual labour was started to be considered as the lowest form of work [while our scriptures consider every work as sacred and important in its place and accept the dignity of labour) consequently a guilt complex and inequity started to prevail in the society. The true lessons taught by our VEDAS, UPNISHADS and BHAGVADGEETA were interpreted wrongly and the whole society has gradually become divided.

The Britishers saw the divided India and destroyed whatever good was left. They associated Indian ethos and values with so many inhuman practices, untouchability and wasteful Vedic rituals etc. and started to look down everything Indian. On the other hand, Indians who got education through English medium also become the victims of this prejudice. They also lost respect for their own national heritage, culture, values, etc.

But now the time has come to research the age-old Vedic values and Indian Ethos and their positive impact on managerial effectiveness. No nation can progress on borrowed culture for all the times. And we do have very rich culture, traditions and values with us. The only thing required is to accept them and try to learn and understand them in their right perspective and then apply them in practice and we would see the wonderful results. Now it is the responsibility to make this change is of the youth. Today's world with its changing economic, political, technological and socio-cultural aspects can be better managed by following Indian values and ethos. Thus, this CHANGE is in right direction that may create management smoodh.

9

LEADERSHIP – AS VIEWED IN GEETA

Leadership plays a significant role in the success story of any organisation. Without appropriate leadership an organisation may end up in confusion and chaos. Leadership is the force to persuade others to seek defined objectives enthusiastically. According to G. R. Terry, Leadership is the activity of influencing people to strive willingly for mutual objectives. In fact, it is leadership which transforms potential into reality.

Thus, managers plan and organise while leaders influence to implement. In a competitive environment of today we need managers who can also be effective leaders.

Western management philosophy gives three major approaches in the area of leadership:

(i) Trait approach,

(ii) Behavioural approach, and

(iii) Situational approach.

In the early days it was believed that leaders are born and not made. Different thinkers have given different in-born qualities which make individuals effective leaders. The qualities or traits referred are courage, willpower, judgement, flexibility, self-confidence, integrity, intelligence, health and physical fitness, vitality, persuasiveness, stability or consistency of behaviour, initiative, moral qualities, enthusiasm, dominance, etc. These qualities make an individual, a leader.

But fifty years' of study (Eugene E. Jennings) has failed to produce a one personality trait of qualities that can be used to discriminate leaders and non-leaders. There is also a problem of measuring traits. And there have been many people with the traits specified for leaders but they were not good leaders. Thus, researchers failed to isolate traits that are strongly associated with successful leadership.

Hence, there evolved behavioural approach. It emphasises that strong leadership is the result of effective role behaviour. Leadership reflects in an individual's behaviour and actions more than in his traits. Thus, when it became evident that effective leaders did not seem to have any distinguishing trait or characteristic, researchers tried to isolate the behaviour that make leaders effective, instead of figuring out what traits effective leaders have. Now more focus began to be given on how they delegate authority, how they distribute tasks, how they communicate, how they provide leadership, how they motivate, how they themselves perform, etc.

After Second World War it has been experienced that a leader successful in one situation failed in another situation which has developed situational approach in leadership.(Churchill, the P M of England was a very successful leader during war, but people have not elected him in next election – perhaps considering that a leader in war may not be successful in peace) Fiedler and Robert House have given their contingency or situational theories in leadership where certain factors associated with different situations have been discussed.

Thus, leaders with some inborn qualities like intelligence, self-confidence, judgement, dominance, discriminating ability, physical features, etc. can learn and acquire some other qualities like technical skills, motivation skills, communication skills, social skills, empathy, objectivity, human relations, emotional stability, etc. to make their leadership behaviour more effective in any given situation. Some of them are.

Communication Skills

Every individual is a unique personality. He brings with him his likes, dislikes, feelings, hopes, aspirations, attitudes, emotions, ideas, fears and what not? Every individual brings his own inner world with him/her into an organisation. This inner world is to be mingled harmoniously with the external world provided by the organisation. Here leader must have a skill to create such an environment in which everyone can express his opinion, doubts and views freely. And this is possible only where no one is considered superior or inferior by the leader, where each job is considered as sacred as any other job, where dignity of labour is accepted, where people feel that they are understood, where persons discover their self-respect and where leader's behaviour does not create any complex in the mind of others. In such environment communication becomes automatically free, open and very smooth and two ways in its true sense. 'Rajarshi' concept can bring all these things.

Decision-making Skill

Decision-making can be divided into two parts. Decision-making process and decision-making itself. Indian philosophy states that the same **Atman** reflects in every living being. All the human beings have divinity and immense potentialities in themselves. Everyone has some creative and innovative skills. Hence, during the process of decision-making the issue under consideration should be discussed with all the concerned people. Their ideas, opinions and suggestions also may prove fruitful; hence thorough attention shall be given to these. After this the leader who is the decision-making authority, takes the decision with confidence that all the people will put their heart into its execution as the decision is not imposed on them. They take the decision as their own, because they also have contributed their share in the decision-making.

Human Relations Skill

Good relations, respect, loyalty, enthusiasm in work, etc. are not to be demanded, they are to be commanded. An individual's sincerity, loyalty, interest in work, initiative, etc. cannot be purchased. They are to win. How? A leader with human relations skill considers employees as human beings and treats them accordingly. He considers every work as important in its place, accept the dignity of labour, listens very patiently and with interest to his followers, provides exemplary conduct, makes people feel that they are understood and taken care of and does not create any complex while communicating to them. All these basic things will lead to better and healthy human relations, essential for managerial excellence.

Conceptual Skill

Apart from all the above skills a leader also requires conceptual skills, organisational effectiveness and managerial excellence. The leader/manager is always required to take right, pragmatic and result-oriented decisions in today's changing environment. This is possible only if he is having a very sound base of theoretical knowledge. Moreover, he must also keep pace with the rapid changes which take place in environmental forces on one hand and expanding horizons of knowledge in his respective area in which he is functioning on the other.

Apart from this some knowledge of Indian values, ethos and culture which have their roots in Indian Philosophy is also equally essential for Indian managers specifically and for the managers all over the world generally as some of these are universal truths, which are very beautifully given in BHAGVADGITA unambiguously with adequate reason and logic. GEETA is not a book or Philosophy which is related to any particular race, age, religion or country. It is for the whole mankind.

If these universal truths described in GEETA are practised by managers, they would not only be able to manage their organisations more effectively with providing successful leadership, but they can also live a meaningful and happy life, free of stress and strain.

In GEETA we found four major qualities required for effective leadership behaviour.

These four qualities are:

(i)   Appropriate conduct

(ii) Emotional maturity

(iii) Self-management

(iv) World-view or Macro vision

(i) Appropriate conduct

In GEETA it is said,

Ydhyedacharati Shrethastattdevetaro Janah |
SA Yatpramanam Kurute Lokastdanuvartate | |

Whatever a leader does, another person does that very thing. Whatever he upholds as authority, an ordinary person follows that.

Leader is he who leads others. Therefore he should be very careful in his thinking, speaking and acting because he is likely to be followed by other people. In all the organisations a person who is at the helm of the organisation, is considered as Srestha. In fact every organisation is having a hierarchy of Sresthas. Every executive who manages some other persons at top, middle and bottom level of management is Shreshta for his subordinates.

Urwick has also stated in one of his books, "It is not what a leader says, still less what he writes, that influences subordinates. It is what he is. And they judge what he is by what he does and how he behaves". Urwick has expressed this view in 20th century while the same was with us in India since centuries together.

Thus, a leader's behaviour should always be an appropriate one. If we take the example of today's most of the politicians and even so-called religious leaders, heads of different departments and institutes, government and semi-government officers, we found most of them totally corrupt, dishonest and irresponsible towards their duty as shresthas. Unfortunately, people look upon them as shresthas, and follow them in whatever they do. And we see that slowly but steadily the whole society is becoming dishonest and insincere in performing the duty. Hence, it is emphasised in GEETA again and again that a leader has a great responsibility and he has to be very careful in his thoughts, speech and deeds because he is always being watched very minutely by others. This is the reason why his behaviour must always be ideal and inspiring for others.

It is our experience that even in the midst of the most corrupt environment if a leader happens to be honest, sincere and totally non-corrupt the whole environment around is affected positively by such an individual's leadership behaviour and pure and powerful character and personality. This we can see at present under the leadership of our P M Narendra Modi in our nation.

Therefore, if a leader starts walking towards righteous path, people will follow him with dedication and respect. Today we found our P. M. Narendra Modi's personality like this. Hence one should not pause to think, but start walking towards the right path and one will surprisingly see oneself followed by many other people. as the leader is like that.

(ii) Emotional Maturity

In GEETA it is said,

Karmnyevadhikaraste Ma Faleshu Kadachit |
Ma Karmfalheturbhurma Te Sangostvakarmani | |

KARMA means in Indian Philosophy, a duty or DHARMA in a given situation. Karma or action or work is very natural for the MAN. Only dead body is non-working.

In the above stanza it is said, "You have choice over your actions but not over the results any time. Do not (take yourself) be the author of the results of action, neither be attached to inaction".

This stanza should not be misunderstood. It does not preach us to perform action without any expectation for results. Performing an action without any expectation is just impossible. There is nothing wrong in having expectations. But one should not indulge into the future expectations, while performing an action so as to affect the very quality of one's performance adversely that may lead to even failure. One should remember that past is dead and future is not yet born, hence, one should concentrate only on present valuable moments for the most efficient performance to get the desired result. Yours jurisdiction is only up to deciding the action.

Result falls into the jurisdiction of the Laws of Nature. And we do not have knowledge about all these laws. The only fact we know is "One cannot avoid the result of one's action," One cannot jump out of window and expect the result-falling-not to happen. It is going to happen according to the law of gravitation which existed even before IZZEK NEWTON invented it. Similarly, you get result of your action according to the Laws of Nature – invented as well as still to be invented – which are the instruments in the hands of Ishvar who gives you the result of your action. Thus, RESULT is an objective reality which should be accepted with equanimity of mind. Success or failure is only subjective perception.

But generally when unexpected and undesired results come, these disturb our mind. We cannot maintain equanimity of mind against unliked results. Consequently, we feel frustration, disappointment, depression or anger. Thus when the unexpected and critical situation expects us to ACT, we only just REACTS and turns the situation into a crisis. You take undesired result as your 'FAILURE' – viewing it from your subjective perception and lose all your effectiveness, efficiency and courage. In fact, when you face unexpected result you need more courage and serenity of mind than a normal situation. Hence, GEETA says to learn to accept result without reaction. This is possible only when you accept your limitations and always be prepared for even the worst situation. Otherwise you as a depressed, frustrated or angry individual will not be able to manage your own self. How can you manage other things? Hence, try to understand the truth.

It will enrich you in experience and you can learn a lot if you accept it with balanced mind. Then your likes and dislikes will no longer be capable of creating any disturbance or reaction in your mind. You will obtain emotional maturity. Then you will become the master of all the situations-favourable or unfavourable. With this equanimity you will be able to face the situation appropriately and manage even a crisis effectively and successfully.

People will appreciate your equanimity of mind and matured personality and follow your leadership with respect and dedication.

Such leaders transform the place of work into a place of worship and create an environment in which individuals, organizations and the whole society can grow and develop.

(iii) Self-management

Before managing people and other things a leader or manager must be able to manage his own SELF. Self-management is considered very important in Indian Philosophy.

What is self-management – is also discussed at different places in GEETA during the discourses between the LORD and ARJUNA. The important lessons taught in GEETA are as under:

A leader must be satisfied with his own self. Otherwise if as leader you are not satisfied with you, then you are required to do something continuously to set things right to make you satisfied. Life will become full of stress and strain. The mind remains agitated and restless all the time. Leaders with such disturbed mind can never be successful leaders.

Similarly, a leader has to learn to accept the outer world also as it is. He should understand that by trying to change the world outside, he will not be happy or satisfied. Instead of it he should change his approach of viewing the world. It is true that if situation can be changed, a leader must have the courage to change it. But if situation cannot be changed, he must also have the courage to accept it and the most important thing that is required on the part of a leader is the intellect to see the difference between the two and act accordingly with equanimity of mind.Apart from this a few other things are also important for managing self.

Practising KARMAYOGA in Life

It has already been mentioned that if one understands that one's jurisdiction is only up to performance of action and result falls in the jurisdiction of laws of nature, then one can perform action with full concentration of mind and intellect and can also accept the result-whatever it may be – with balanced mind.

Maintaining Equanimity of Mind against the Pair of Opposites

The leader must also have learned an art of living a life successfully against the pair of opposites like pain and pleasure, gain and loss, conquest and defeat success and failure etc. by cultivating Ishwararpan and Prasad Buddhi.

Experience gained from any situation favourable or unfavourable will definitely enrich one's life. Such attitude will bring wonderful results. You will be able to accept even the worst situation with courage and equanimity of mind. You will also be able to manage the situation effectively and successfully showing perfect maturity of mind. People will appreciate your capability to tackle the situation with calmness of mind.

Thus, managing self is considered very important in Indian Philosophy. Topical problems come and go and challenges also will always be there in today's changing environment. These can be handled better if one has a well-managed self and mind that is not pre-occupied with fears and doubts about the result, that is calm, matured and awake, that learns from every experience and becomes more and more matured.

(iv) World Vision or Macro Vision

Generally, most of the people suffer from micro vision and self-cantered views in life and behave accordingly and suffer so many problems and conflicts. Instead of this we need to develop macro vision to manage today's world and provide effective leadership.

Such macro vision is taught in GEETA. It says that the man should understand the truth that I am not a single solitary individual. I am a part of the whole universe. And the universe is nothing but the manifestation of the ISHVAR in different forms and figures. Just as the waves rise in the ocean, play in the ocean and disappear into the ocean, the whole universe arises in HIM, exists in HIM and disappears in HIM. As a wave is not different from the ocean, individuals are not different from the whole universe. As a water is the essence of a wave and the ocean, ATMAN is the essence of every individual and the whole universe or BRAHMAND.

Thus, all of us are inter-related with one-another and every one of us has certain role to play, certain responsibilities to exercise.

A question may arise, why I should develop macro vision? Why I should feel one with others who seem different and separate from me? Well, what is about different limbs of your body? These limbs are of different shapes and have different functions. But in fact, these all limbs are you because you live in them. Their joys are your joys and their sorrows are your sorrows. Similarly, the whole universe (Brahmanda) is one mighty expression of the divine spirit of existence. Where you can see the

ONENESS. Even the nuclear scientist, Schrodinger has accepted that 'Consciousness' (Atman or Awareness) has no plural. It is only ONE."

Developing such macro vision is the NEED of today's world.

Thus today we need macro vision intensively but it does not develop on its own. It has to be cultivated. Hard effort is required on the part of a leader who develops such vision within him and who can cultivate the same vision among other people. The Lord brought such vision in Arjuna during HIS discourses in GEETA. The Lord did not alter the situation. He did not offer any position, power of wealth, etc. as motivation to Arjuna. He merely listened to him patiently, talked to him peacefully, answered all his queries, removed his mental confusion and doubts and lifted him out of his micro state of thinking to macro state and made him to see the same problem on a bigger canvas.

If a leader such macro vision, he can lead the people successfully and effectively. Not only will this but he be able to safeguard the interest of not only his own people and organisation, society and his country but the whole world.

Thus from GEETA we can evolve a unique theory of leadership based on four major qualities—(i) Exemplary conduct, (ii) Emotional maturity, (iii) Self-management, and (vi) Macro vision. This theory of leadership is applicable in all kinds of situations, places and times and hence it is universal theory. The leaders have only to acquire these four qualities and they can provide effective leadership by becoming the Master of all the situations at all times and at all the places.

What Bhagwan wants to say – is that every one of us is Shreshtha in one's own place for some others. You may be the Shreshtha for your younger sister and brother, your parents and your grandpa may be Shreshtha for you. Even among your friend-circle you may be considered a leader. Actually in today's organizations at every level you may have a few people working under you. And for them you may be the Shreshta by your exemplary leadership, by your interaction with your men etc. So wherever you are, if you are as Shreshta from some others you must be very careful and alert in your behaviour, the way in which you acts and reacts and in everything.

Here Bhagwan says to Arjuna, you are the leader and the prince like personality and very brave Yoddha. People look up to you for g gaining motivation and if you think to run away then what impression will they have for you? So do your niyat karma. Look at me. Bhagwan gives his own example by saying that I have nothing to gain in all the lokas, and then even I am active. Why? Because If I don't do any Karma then people also will do the same as they consider me the Shreshtha. So the persons whom others look as their inspiration, as their role model, as the Shreshtha, Should be very careful in whatever then say, or act. They must be one in MANA, VACHAN and KARMA, Arjuna, Bhagwan says," You are like that one to whom all these people follow, whatever you say or do, people will follow you. So be strong, stand up and prove that you are the Shreshtha".

Always remember, whatever Bhagwan says to Arjuna applies to all of us. Never try to run away from the situation. Face it bravely and if you are the Shreshtha even for 3-4 persons, your responsibility increases. Play your role as expected.

10

MOTIVATION: A NEW DIMENSION

Thinkers in western world define motivation in different ways. In all the definitions motivation is explained as a process that stimulates people to perform better, to accomplish desired organisational goals. In the early days classical thinkers considered "MONEY" as a motivating factor. Man was considered as an "ECONOMIC MAN". F.W. Tailor stated that "Man will not do an extra ordinary day's work for an ordinary day's pay". His principles of scientific management were meant for higher productivity through financial incentives.

Then neo-classical thinkers developed two approaches: Human relations approach and Behavioural approach. Under human relations approach it was believed that keeping relations good and keeping employees happy make them perform better. Their assumption was "happy workers are more productive". This all thinking was based on the conclusions drawn from Hawthorne Experiments during 1930s and 1940s. But later on some experiments showed that happy workers are not necessarily more productive. Productivity does not depend solely on happiness and 'satisfaction of employees. It depends on so many other factors like quality of technology, organisational effectiveness, plant efficiency, quality of leadership etc. Apart from this it was accepted that productivity depends on how the managers behave with people, how he deals with the situations, how he empowers the personnel and how he motivates the employees. Thus, behavioural approach became popular, During those days Mc Gregor, Maslow, Herzberg, McClleland; Vroom etc have given their motivation theories.

These all theories considered MAN as an "Administrative man", who does not emphasise only "money" as a reward for his performance at work. Other factors like social and psycological aspects, esteem and self actualisation aspects of needs also became equally important or more important than money. Later on individual's ability, talent, skill, his expectation for his performance also were considered important for motivation. Thus, the development of the concept of motivation continued. The modern thinkers believe that "MAN" is very complex to understand and to motivate him by using any of motivation techniques/theories is not that simple.

Sophocles has described a "MAN" rightly in following words:

"The wonder of wonders is MAN; Man is the most dynamic being. He has an infinite capability to think, to create, to develop, to discover and invent, to produce, to feel, to love, to dream, to conquer, to master, to achieve, to give, to respect, to play, to pray, and to do as well as to destroy, to hate and to kill. He is the most complex being".

This is the "MAN" at work in the present scenario that management wants to motivate successfully. First let it be made clear what is the present Scenario?

We are passing through revolutionary changes around us since last 2-3 decades. The world has been transferring into a very big village, as in a small village one knows everything about everybody, One has become now capable to know everything that happens in any corner of the world thanks to the revolutionary changes in our telecomunication systems including Inter-net etc.

Earlier working force was generally classified into two categories: White colour jobs and blue–colour jobs. And most of the motivation theories were applied to motivate blue-colour jobs. But now the number of blue–colar jobs which was 88 percent in 1960s, have been reduced to 17 percent in 1990s due to technological revolution and will further dwindle to 2 Percent in 2025 A.D. (Times of India Ahmadabad, 18-4-1995) And gradually it may reduce to less than 1 to 2 Percent by the time 2050 A. D.

In 20th century capitalists were putting their capital for productive use and they were dominating the world. Now with management revolution in 21st century "Knowledge Professionals" will put knowledge to productive use and they will dominate the world. Drucker says, yesterday management/society was divided between capitalist (MALIK) and proletariat (SHARMIK). Tomorrow the same management is going to be divided between "knowledge workers" and "service workers". At the top level management, 20 percent "knowledge personnel" will conceive new ideas, new concepts, new products, new vision etc. They are "thinking" personnel and 80 percent service personnel will execute and implement their ideas and materialise their visions and dreams.

Thus the work force will be more informed, skilled, trained and knowledgeable. We cannot apply the popular motivation theories as they are to motivate them. Apart from this management has also to learn to motivate in midst of diversity and multiculturalism in the present scenario.

Multiculturalism as it applies to management can be defined as—there are many different cultural backgrounds and factors which have become important in organisations and that people from different backgrounds can coexist and flourish within an organisation, if properly understood and dealt with in right perspective. Usually, multiculturalism refers to certain cultural factors such as gender, ethnicity, race, religion, language, social customs, traditions, life styles etc. Hence, management has to evolve new ways to motivate employees under multicultural management, where it has to learn to accommodate varying interest of different cultural groups of people and try to understand the needs of diverse groups and provide motivation accordingly.

Let us have a look into some such multicultural factors which need management's attention for motivating concerned personnel effectively:

(1) Increasing Number of Women:

One important change that we experience since last 2-3 decade is the increasing number of women not only in advanced countries but also in developing countries. Management must accept the fact that women are coming with talent, skill and different approaches to their jobs and relationships and talent is gender blind, colour blind and has nothing to do with race, religion or language. These women have begun to redefine their roles in the society. The work force will no remain male dominated in 21st century. How to motivate these women? It is very important problem. By considering the problems they face and some barriers and hindrances they have to suffer during their career only management can motivate them. Women generally face the problems of unequal treatrnent, inadequate opportunities and problems related to family and children. Management should accept the fact that women will be more and more career oriented and they will demand equal career advancement opportunities. They rightly argue that only qualifications, competence, talent and capability should be considered in giving higher managerial positions and also in junior positions at middle level management. If women are fully competent, qualified, career oriented and experienced, they can be motivated to continue their job and to reach higher positions by excellent performance in due course of time by helping them in achieving their goals. Management can help women employees to resolve work and family conflicts with job sharing, compressed work weeks, flexible work schedule and other such programmes in order to motivate them and increase their productivity and reduce their turnover rate. Thus here the way in which management can motivate in next millennium is quite different.

(2) Issue of Language:

Language is another factor which splits some nations into more than one culture, In Belgium there are two cultures based on two languages: French & Dutch. In Switzerland also there are two cultures matching its two languages Germen & French. In Canada also two languages are spoken English and French. In India also there are many languages. In the process of globalisation the number of MNCs is also increasing. And people belonging to different countries and different cultures have to work together. During interaction language becomes a problem. If two countries speak the same language then even British and American English are often miles apart. If you tell someone his presentation was "Quite good" an American will be happy but British will ask you, "What was wrong with it? Thus, management will be required to motivate concerned personnel to learn more than one or two languages.

(3) Job Enrichment:

Apart from spoken language sometimes unspoken language and some gestures create confusion. Herzberg has given the concept of job enrichment years before. At that time he was criticised that by job enrichment only non managerial personnel can be motivated. So far as manager is concerned, his job itself is challenging which motivates himself. He does not require any external motivation by enriching job etc. But in next millennium if enough information is provided about the explicit and implicit meaning of certain terms and gestures in different languages and cultures then managers also feel comfortable and motivated. For example, Japanese people never say 'No' as it is considered offensive and rude in their culture. They avoid saying 'No' at any cost. To the unknowing American the unwillingness to say 'No' in clear terms mean that there is 'hope'. But Japanese listen politely and then respond with 'Hai'. Literally that means yes but usually it only means, "I hear you". That is all. Hence it is to be understood that when Japanese try to avoid saying yes or No, he wishes to say 'No'. If managers do not know this fact they feel much embarrassment. They feel uncomfortable. Here management can motivate managers by providing them facilities to learn such things related to other languages or cultures. Motorola in the U. S. has already used this tool with success. It has motivated managers to learn other languages and related cultures. Such kind of motivation we need in 21st century which will increase managers' confidence and they can deal with people belonging to different cultures and speaking different languages comfortably and confidently.

(4) Religion:

Religion is also very important factor. To understand relationship between religion and work related values is not that easy. But it is to be accepted that management has to consider religion related traditions and rituals, while managing diversity. Management has to learn to respect these rituals and then only it can motivate concerned personnel. For example prior to doing business in Saudi Arabia, Management should remember that these is the predominance of Islam and Muslims pray five times a day, have strict regulations regarding drugs, alcohol and about women too. If management is doing business with Indians, it can win their love and co-operation if it celebrates some of their important religious events and respects their values and norms. Thus motivation is becoming situational. Any readymade model or theory will not work in 21st century.

(5) Existence of Racial and Ethnic Minority:

Racial and Ethnic minority groups have also their significance. Many cultural differences exist between ethnic minority groups like, Africans, Asians (Including Indians) Americans, and Latins etc. All these people while working in MNCs especially away from their home country experience and feel challenges and stress if they think their own cultural heritage was devalued and then they will be demotivated. Hence management should consider the issue seriously and make required changes in its attitude and approach towards these people otherwise management will not get benefits out of the investments they made in their human resources.

Most of the organisations in global economy have now realised that such diversity exists and that the management must pay the attention to the needs of sets of very diverse employees. This is essential if managers want to motivate and lead successfully different cultures in the competitive global market.

India is also multi lingual, multi ethnic and multi cultural society and seeks competitive advantage in global economy. But in the midst of such vast diversity India has also developed some homogeneity of values and beliefs among its people. Two common characteristics of Indian culture are continuity of religious beliefs and hierarchical nature of social structure. American psychologist Alan Rotand (1988) has said that Indians are strongly family and caste oriented and religious by nature. This information is necessary not only for MNCs operating in India but for Indian companies too. They can capitalise on this information and accordingly can conclude 3 major aspects of Indian culture: (i) Personalised Relationship, (ii) Family orientation and (iii) Religious orientation. While influencing people's behaviour or motivating people in desired direction if management remembers these three features of Indian culture it can motivate personnel successfully.

Thus, present scenario reflects revolutionary changes in all the fields. Moreover markets are becoming more and more global and competitive. Complex and variable business environment is becoming more and more risky and full of uncertainty. In such scenario of this millennium there will not be any job security. An individual has to prove his efficiency and competence by his performance not for only his career advancement or growth but even for survival. In these circumstances every individual will be motivated to perform better. His inner wisdom will direct him. No external motivation tools and techniques will work.

Further, in the early days it was believed that personal contact is very important to motivate people and we were used to give the example of Henry Ford, Robert Owen etc. But now the situation is inside out. Until recently when you worked with someone it meant you were both in the same place. You met each other, had a cup of tea and lunch together, had meetings to brain storm and even to socialise. Now in this information era this is no longer true. You chat, mail, confer and work together with someone for years without having met or even talked personally to him. In this situation. Where motivation is to be placed?

Apart from this organisations have been becoming horizontal. All hierarchies are being broken. Organisations form the teams of the individuals drawn from different areas. These teams work autonomous. Even within the teams each individual becomes a distinct unit. Top level management put forward the vision and goals,. The teams work for realising these. Hence, they foster a spirit of entrepreneurship in the team-members which is very important. Each individual is a distinct unit with separate cost and profit head. In this scenario work itself becomes a motivator and a leader. Once mission is given people know what is expected of them. Leadership is informed and shared, and most often team members are leaders at one or other point of the process. The question therefore is where we are going to place motivation in this scenario?

Thus, in revolutionary changed scenario of 21st century motivation no longer will remain external as it was thought in 20th century by western management thinkers. It has to be internal. Every individual will have to perform his/her best not only for the survival of his job but also for his own growth and development, for getting higher positions and for his own satisfaction in tomorrow's extra-ordinary competitive market.

Here we take pride in noting that according to Indian Philosophy motivation was never considered external. It remains always "INTERNAL" in our culture. The whole world scenario has changed in such a manner that motivation is no more remain external.

Now let it be explained that how motivation is internal according to our culture. You and I are alive. Therefore we cannot but active. Only thing that is required to understand by the management is how the actions can be organised, altered or disciplined for achieving organisational goals and how to create a sense of satisfaction and fulfilment in the individuals. This job is to be performed by the leaders and Indian Philosophy gives the unique idea of leadership which directs peoples through its exemplary behaviour, Rajarshi quality, emotional maturity and understanding of Karmayoga. Moreover work is considered the only means into the hands of individual's growth and development in Indian philosophy. If man does not work, he has no further opportunity to develop. Further work is considered as DUTY which is to be performed by the individual in a given situation. A student has his duty, a teacher has his duty, a son has his duty, parents have their duty and employees and managers have also their duty, Duty is defined as DHARM and it is to be performed through Karma/action. Hence there is no difference between **Karma & Dharm** in our culture. Thus every one works and performs one's duty. What matters is how to perform the work and with what attitude one should work.

The great sages of ancient Indian observed that the quality of work that people perform can be classified in to three categories: The first is the lowest type of work which is performed only for the sake of wages, profit, personal gain and benefits. The most of the western motivation theories which try to induce people for better performance by offering them money, power, position etc. produce such kind of people. The second is the work performed for some ideal with eyes not on personal profit but on well-being of the society as a whole. Here people are inspired by great enthusiasm and great vision of life. Here the individual is ready to suffer and sacrifice for his ideal. Our young boys and girls including Bhagatsingh, Rajyaguru, Sukhdev, Chandrashekar etc. who have laid their lives for the freedom of our country belong to this category. The third variety is of the men of achievement. Though few in number, these people give a fillip to the general cultural beauty of society and uplift the entire generation. Such mighty individuals are men/women of great virtues and values. They inspire people even after their death. Buddha, Christ, Shankaracharya, Mahatma Gandhi, Vivekananda, worked in the world not for profits or any personal gains but from a feeling that they are doing the right thing and that was their DUTY in given situation irrespective of whether or not they will be recognised in their life time. They find joy and satisfaction in their work.

Among these three categories the 2nd and 3rd category need no motivation. In the case of lst category to which most of the people belong management is required to create such an environment where people will be motivated internally. If we consider Maslow's theory, it seems that man is basically a needy animal. But Indian culture considers all human beings as children of immortal bliss **(Amrutasya Putraha)** and full of immense potentialities. But sometimes we are not able to reflect or make use of these immense capabilities.

As we fail to remove their doubts, anxieties, confusion, and wrong thinking. Arjuna was motivated from the very beginning but he lost his motivation due to some obstacles, hurdles and confusion in his mind. All that was required was only to remove these obstacles. Thus removing obstacles during the performance of job is motivation in Indian philosophy. A very appropriate example can be given here to make this clearer. A piece of sandal wood, kept in water for a long period of time, smells bed, but if it is cleared then the sweet fragrance will come out naturally. For bringing out its original fragrance we have to remove obstacles only. Similarly every individual has immense potentialities. Management has only to bring out that potentiality by removing obstacles, fears, hurdles, doubts etc. Such motivation involves inner beauty and does not promote any greed in an individual to have more and more in return of his work.

Moreover, in present scenario to manage the diversity successfully management need only an understanding and care of different cultures with all their related aspects. Traditional theories which try to motivate people by external stimuli will not work there. Bhagvadgeeta is a story of motivation. In 1st chapter Arjuna decided not to fight and put his arguments in 19 shlokas. Shri Krishna did not interrupt and gave patient listening. When Arjuna completed, Lord Krishna started speaking. He first appealed him on the emotional level, then on intellectual level and showed how to look at the problem on a bigger canvas.

Then he gave action plan and also showed the results of his action plan. As a result, Arjuna who has told him in the beginning that "I will not fight" (means I will not perform my action/duty) tells him at the end that "I will do what you say". This is a very wonderful story of motivation where motivation was internal. Motivated he was from the very beginning but due to some doubts and confusion in his mind he was reluctant in performing his duty. When doubts were cleared he said, "I will perform my duty".

Similarly in today's world and in the world of tomorrow individual will always be internally motivated. He wants to perform his best in his own interest. But sometimes he may face some problems, some doubts in his mind, some confusions and obstacles that may restrict him to perform satisfactorily. Here management all over the world has to accept that in tomorrow's world only the Indian concept which states that motivation is internal will work where management has only to identify the doubts, problems and obstacles in the environment of diversity and try to remove them and the individuals who are educated trained, skilled, informed and experienced who are in fact, knowledge workers will shine out in their performance in relative areas. This will be the understanding of the concept of motivation in the next millennium

Lord Krushna motivated Arjuna successfully by this technique of motivation. In fact the Geeta is a story of motivation where Arjuna in the beginning says, 'I will not fight "and at the end he says "I will do what you say. "Arjuna was not offered any position etc. for this but all the obstacles have been removed. Motivated he was from the beginning. He only required some of his wrong thiking cleared.

Here Geeta shows five stages of motivation

1—Patience listening—Here Bhagwan Krushna did not interrupt Arjuna and gave patience listening where Arjuna puts his problems from 29 to 47 verses in the first chapter of Geeta.

2—Putting stress on good points/strength while removing Arjuna's doubts.

3—Discussing on intellectual level-showing the essence of Karma/Duty

4—Showing the action plan to achieve the goal.

5—Discussing the consequences of proposed action plan.

Thus Bhagvadgeeta teaches how to motivate the individual within. To understand this in its right sense some basic concepts of Indian philosophy need some deliberation

The first is the unique concept of work in Vedanta where work is considered as duty or dharma. Non working body is dead body. The man has to work for his own growth and development. An Indian does not work only for his livelihood but he works as it is the only means available to him to manifest whatever divinity and potentiality and creativity he has within.

But it does not mean that Indians have no needs to satisfy. Needs are there. They also work to satisfy them but the objectives and ways in which actions are performed are quite different.

Under our philosophy needs fall into three categories.

1 Need for existence—SAT.

These needs include physiological, safety and security needs given by Maslow. Vedanta describes this need in its unique way. It describes it as a strong desire in man to perpetuate his existence. This is a natural desire. Everyone wants to remain alive. No one wants to die. All the means of security, good job, good salary, safety that he surrounds himself with shelter, comforts etc. are all with a view to continue life as long as possible. This desire is love for life or immortality and man works for satisfying this desire. Management can help them to provide the means for that and they will work for manifesting what talent and potentiality they have within. To make them work no external motivation is required

2 Needs for knowledge—CHIT.

No one can stand ignorance. The man wants to know everything. We want to know what is there on the Moon, on the sun and what is there in different planets.This love for knowledge in every one of us is natural desire.

That is why I can do away with breakfast in the morning but I must have a news paper every morning. FOR THIS MANAGEMENT SHOULD PROVIDE all the necessary information about not only for its own organisation, its policies,plans,programs, etc.to the employees and keep them informed about the happenings in their unit but also give them opportunities to develop themselves to keep upto date their knowledge in their respective areas. Thus it can be a very powerful means for motivation.

3 Desire for Happyness;

Third desire is to gain happiness in life and this is basic desire and also a natural desire.Thus by continuing the existence longer and by getting knowledge the man wans to gain only happiness.

How these desires can be satisfied?

Vedic Vision shows four means; Artha, Kama, Dharma and Moksha.

First thing man will try to get in his life is food, clothing and shelter.These are the basic necessities of life for existence.Apart from this the man wants to acquire the things which he does not have [YOGA] and wants also to protect those things which he already have. [KSHEME]These are the desires felt at physiological level.

When physical needs satisfied, there arise the needs of mind, desire for mental pleasure.These are described as KAMA in INDIAN PHILOSOPHY.

Under ARTHA man seeks happiness at the level of body.[existence] Under KAMA he seeks pleasure at mental level.But still he is not satisfied. Now he wants power,position name and fame,respect and recognition. Nothing wrong in it.But these all things are to be achieved by proper ways and means-based on values and DHARMA.Apart from this Dharma also means good deeds for the others,for the society-known as Punya Karma.

Inspite of all such achievements Man still wants something special. He does not know what he wants but he is not happy with what he has.In fact he wants that happiness which is eternal and not limited by time place or object.Upnishads describe it as limitless happiness.Basically all of us want peace, harmony and happiness inside.This is possible only when we have no more worldly desires.And this is described in our vedic vision as a desire to be free from all the desires to acquire worldly gains-that is shown as MOKSHA,which is placed at the highest level of needs.

Maslow describes his Need Hierarchy Theory and goes upto the level of self actualisation need.Though Maslow also explained later on 'transcendence of ego, selfishness, ego centering etc.'He also further added that 'when one is doing one's duty, this also can be seen to be under the aspect of eternity and can represent a transcendence of the ego of the lower needs of the self.'He describes this as a form of meta motivation

Vedant philosopphy goes one step ahead and states a need for achiveing limitless happiness.. It further states that this is as natural as physiological needs and mental needs are. And every natural desire in this universe does have a solution. For example hunger and thirst are natural desires so food and water is provided by the nature. We are not talking here about the cultivated desires.Seking happiness which is a basic desire in man is natural and it must have a solution. But man seeks that happiness in money, power. Position, entertainment, name and fame and fails to find it there.

So when we say that we want to get rid of motality, ignorance and unhappiness or sorrow, it indicates that these things are not natural to us..We never complain,'Doctor, please do something because my eyes see'as it is natural..

Therefor all our limitations we feel in our life about mortality, ignorance and sorrorw are unnatural. In fact Immortaslity. Kmowledge and happiness are natural to me. I am sat, chit and anand.

Thus the oblective of our every activity is to obtain that happiness.And external means of motivation can not bring the limitless happiness what the Man actually wants. Because we apply limited means to get unlimited happiness.Money,other financial means or even postion, promotion are not enough to get limitless happiness. When this fact is realised by man he can be described as a matured and enlightened Man.

Thus such understanding brings positive outlook towards oneself, towards his work, and towards others. Such people become self motivated persons. They do not requre any extrovert incentives. Work itself is a motivating force for them.

Apart from this, as we have seen ealier Karmayoga also plays an important role in motivating people where they concentrate on their work fully and not having any worry about the result as they know that it is not their jurisdiction.So they can perform their job without any attachment towards results and accept results as they are, with equanimity of mind and without any reaction. Such men do not need any external motivation. And they can also place the process at the right track by correcting the loopholes.

Karmayogis can do this and the world needs such an attitude of Karmayoga in the current scenario...where motivation is internal. This is our Vedic thinking that reflects in Geeta.

11

STRESS MANAGEMENT (WORK-CULTURE AND ATTITUDE)

Managers, executives and then most of the persons working on top or of middle level in any organisation experience stress due to a large number of factors. They have to work in a target oriented area where deadlines are given and have to perform under Conflicting situations in the midst of increasing competition at national as well as international 1evel. Moreover, they have to deal with so many people and things at a time. And along with their own personal goals they are required to fulfil their task-goals and organisational goals.

Their mind, therefore, remains always under stress. Anxiety, fear, frustration, demanding situations, uncertainty, conflict in relationships, challenges, high ambition etc. create stress in the mind of persons concerned.

Stress is generally attributed to external factors and hence most of the workshops and seminars on stress-management lay emphasis on developing skill and strategies to deal with these external factors. But researchers now accept that stress results from a combination of a vast number of factors – internal, i.e. associated with the individual's personality and external over which the man hsa to control.

Significant studies were conducted by Friedman and Rosemen and they found two types of personalities from the point of view of stress. Type A personality is generally aggressive, ambitious with an air of supreme self-confidence and absorbed in the work exclusively. Persons with such personality are workaholic. Against this the type B personality is less ambitious, easy going and more laid back in his attitude to work. Looking to the qualities of these two types of personalities, Type A personalities are more susceptible to stress and therefore to high-blood pressure, increased Cholesterol levels, heart disease and other stress related illness. People belonging to type A personality are typically aggressive, competitive, impatient, hostile to frustration and possess a very strong sense of time urgency. While type B personalities are exactly the opposite. They do not get agitated, they can relax and hence comparatively able to cope with stress.

Thus, a person with type A personality disposition is likely to experience more stress than a Type B personality. In fact, most of the individuals have both – type A and Type B – personality traits with different degrees of mix of the two. If you have more of the characteristics of Type A personality, you are likely to be more stress-prone.

Stressors are of two kinds – Interpersonal and organisational. Stresses caused due to poor working relationship, group conflicts, lack of trust, role ambiguity and poor relationships with peers and subordinates are described as interpersonal stresses. It is to be emphasised here that a healthy work-environment with able leadership and skillful team building causes very little interpersonal stress. Whatever stress exists in such healthy work environment is related to team-performance which plays a positive role within an organisation. Healthy environment depends on supportive leadership, mutual trust and cooperation.

Organisational stresses are caused due to the lack of proper systems, and guidance, lack of fairness in Salary structure, under-load or Overload work situations, lack of adequate authority, too much travelling and other environmental factors. Apart from these stress may also be due to the private life problems. Experts on stress management are of the view that a lot of stress may be due to the demands placed on time and finance from family, relatives and community. Moreover rising prices and increased family demands also cause stress in case of a fair number of middle level executives. At a higher level, ambition of achieving too much in too short a time causes stress in individual life.

However, stress also has a positive impact. Stress sometimes proves as an asset so long as it is manageable and helps in creating healthy competition. Many of the organisational excellence and individual successes are achieved through well-managed stresses.

Moreover, a stress-free life is not possible in today's environment – not only for executives but students and women – who manage only their study and home. All that we can do is to manage it well to keep it to a reasonable level where it can play a positive role.

It is difficult to suggest a universal and well-integrated comprehensive system of stress management, as every organisation has a unique environment and every individual has a unique personality. However, western management philosophy gave some suggestions to maintain stress at some reasonable level – which is given below in brief.

- Delegating authority adequately.

- Accepting the principle of exception.

- Developing a second line of command.

- Building trust.

- Changing the attitude to view the situation. For example, thinking about unfinished tasks as initiated tasks.

- Setting realistic objectives.

- Learning methods of relaxation.

- Taking up some hobbies.

- Managing time properly – etc. etc.

Bhartiya vision also has a unique system of stress management. It also accepts Anxiety, fear, demanding situations, conflict, and uncertainty ete. Cause stress and it also has its own way of managing stress.

First, it states that 'work' is very much natural for a human being. A living body has no alternative but to work. Moreover it also states that every human being has the element of divinity within him. Men are children of bliss. For bringing out that divinity the Man works and work is "SADHNA" in Bhartiya Philosophy. Geeta also states that when work is considered as duty, there comes attitudinal change in the performance of a work. Consequently, performance of duty with this understanding is always a matter of joy and satisfaction as one performs one's Swadharma and not a matter of Compulsion or boredom.

Moreover, it teaches that you are Atman and not a body, mind or intellect (that actually performs a work) generally sense of doership creates stress because then only the feelings like "I failed", "I succeed" etc. arises. But with the true understanding of 'Atman', if the sense of doership is 1eft out, stress will reduce or cease to exist.

It is a fact that a successful endeavour of any undertaking involves not only one's own effort, but also so many other factors controllable as well as non-controllable. Therefore if things do not happen according to one's expectations, one should accept the reality without giving any reaction with maturity of mind. Apart from this Geeta and our scripturls state one wonderful thing that I possess nothing. Everything I possess, skill, talent, intelligence, capability, body, mind etc. are given to me for "USE". If we take all these things as "MINE" and "Ours' ', failure and success, sorrow and joy will also become 'Ours' and then these will affect us and create fear, tension and frustration, resulting in stress. But if one performs one's duty (work) without any sense of doership, as an offering to the alter of the Almighty, it wil1 not result in any kind of stress. Then I can offer even my failure to the Almighty God with the evenness of mind and with the same ease at which I might have offered my success to "HIM ".

Moreover, our Bhartiya Philosophy also states that result depends on the quality of work. The cause never fails to create an equivalent result/effect. Science also accepts the fact. One should understand that success and failure are the two kinds of results of action. But ideas and perceptions of success and failure are arbitrary concepts created by us only. In fact, these are subjective matters. It is emphasised. in Vedic philosophy that the 'result' is objective reality but to see it as a failure or success is subjective reality. It is our own perceptions based on our wrong way to look at the results.

The essence of all this thinking is that I should feel bad only if I have not performed action with full concentration, dedication and Commitment, as it is my duty to perform my work in the best possible manner. Moreover I can only determine my action and also quite free to decide whether to perform or not to perform or how to perform that action. But I cannot determine the result thereof. Then how can I be responsible for the things which I have not determined? I should never consider myself responsible for the things which are not under my control and feel stress and make Life dreadful by inviting so many diseases caused by stress. No doubt, I can learn from my failure, I can improve my performance, I can work hard with more sincerity, I can change my way of working to make it more effective. These things are under my control. I can determine these things. But I have no control over the results of my actions and therefore I have to accept them with equanimity of mind.

Such thinking will be helpful to both kind of personalities – Type A and Type B – but Type A personality will be Benefited more as it is more aggressive and agitating and hence more stress-prone.BhartiyaPhilosophy gives four major lessons or guidelines for stress-management.

(A) Accept yourself as you are:

Individuals have to learn to accept themselves as they are with all of their Strength and weaknesses and try to exploit strength and overcome the weaknesses. Most of the problems arise because you are not Satisfied and acceptable to you. In that case you try to get power, position, wealth, name and fame by thinking that these will make you happy and satisfied. But in fact, these things will not give you satisfaction. You will remain continuously under stress and strain to get more and more of it. Happyness, in fact, is the very nature of the Atman. Hence look for happiness within. If your mind is not okay, if it is agitated, disturbed and dissatisfied, nothing can give you happiness. So keep your mind calm and peaceful by accepting you as you are and be satisfied with what you are and what you have, because Vedic philosophy believes that life does not begin with birth or ends with death. Life is a Continuum of actions and reactions carried out. Moreover any effect cannot exist without a cause. It is scientific truth. Hence, accept yourself as you are and what you have as an effect which must have its roots in some causes in the near or distant past – in your Innumerable past janma. By accepting these basic things in life you can enjoy your life stress-free.

(B) Accept the world outside as it is:

Sometimes adverse Situations and circumstances in the world and working with careless, insincere and dishonest personnel also create stress and tension. Here Vedic Philosophy states that do not blame the people around you, or the government, society, workers, subordinates etc. for your problems and failure. Accept the situation with Maturity and equanimity of mind. Then only you will be able to find a way out. The ATMAN is the one and the same Atman in all of them. But just as the sunlight reflects itself differently in a pot of clean water and in a pot of dirty water, the same Atman reflects itself differently in a man with purity of mind and with impurity of mind. But remember Ishvar resides in every one of us. Hence do not complain or grumble. Accept everything as it is. Though a man is basically divine by nature, he seems the bundle of good and bad elements. Hence it becomes the duty of every leader to bring out that divinity of him. It is his major duty. such thinking will definitely bring a basic change in one's mental attitude in viewing the others and world outside and the man will be able to perform his duty with a calm mind and can live a stress-free life.

(C) Perform your work–considering it your duty:

As stated earlier, 'work' is considered as 'SADHNA' or Dharma (DUTY) in Vedic philosophy. Work is considered as an exercise of energy. And since I am not the creator of the energy that enables me to work, it is not proper to measure the returns to my efforts only in terms of rewards I get. Here my work can only be an offering to the divine within me/to the Almighty God. Such a concept of work helps to develop humility and reduces the sense of 'doership' and 'I-ness'. It will also heIp in developing divine qualities in human beings along with the skill of managing others. Managers become RAJARSI in the real sense of the word. They can then perform their work/ duty at ease without having any kind of stress and enjoy a meaningful life.

(D) Understand the term KARMAYOGA and exercise it:

If KARMAYOGA is understood in its true sense, it alone can make the man's life stress-free. KARMAYOGA described in Geeta states that do your work with full concentration and dedication without having any anxiety of attachment for results.

The famous Stanza of BhagvadEita states:

KARMANYE VADHIARSTE MA PHALESU
KADACHANA |
MA KARMAPHALA HETURBHURMATE SANGO STV
AKARMANI | |

(Bhagvadgeeta II-47)

The above stanza does not preach us to perform action without any expectation for results. Managers and all of us do have some expectation from our work but they should not indulge into future expectations while performing the action so as to affect the very quality of their performance leading sometimes to total failure.

Only thing to be remembered is that every action ends in a reaction/result. Hence when unexpected results come, it should not disturb your mind. You should not consider yourself as a failure because the result is an objective reality but failure or success is subjective perception. Result is always inherent in action itself and it is also affected by so many other forces, unknown and uncontrollable. Yes, you should plan and execute your work with full concentration and perfect dedication considering even the future implications of current decisions in detail but at the same time your mind should not be anxious for results and preoccupied with fears and doubts about results at the time of actual performance. Such anxieties and fears cause unnecessary stress and strain and even affect the quality of performance adversely. Apart from the youth in job, The students should also remember this while giving an examination.

Therefore you have to learn to accept the result with equanimity of mind. Accept the pairs of opposites like gain and loss, success and failure, pleasure and pain etc. with maturity of mind – The results come from the Laws of Nature/Ishvar (Creator of these Laws) in return of your actions which you have offered to Him. Hence accept them too as they are-as 'Prasad' from Him

Such thinking will definitely help in controlling stress. In fact, stress is the product of emotions and project of imaginations. It is the result of not understanding the realities which can be dealt with appropriately with the proper knowledge and proper understanding of realities, If you are fortunate enough to have such true understanding, you will find that the stress felt by you is your own creation out of wrong thinking and wrong imaginations. If the lessons taught by our own scriptures – especially Geeta are accepted, life can be more joyful, stress-free and meaningful for all of us in any area of activity.

12

MANAGING MIND/SELF

A human being is basically a body-mind complex. We take care of our body in various ways like by taking a daily bath, giving it nutritious food, giving it exercise it needs, giving it required rest etc. But what do we do about our mind? Have you ever thought about it? The mind meets so many accidents daily. It gets hurt, it gets angry, restless, agitated, rejected, disappointed etc. What do we do to take care of our mind? We just do nothing. On the other hand we know that calm, unperturbed, balanced and matured mind is very important to make the right choice or right decision. If you are emotionally upset, your skill, your knowledge, even your experience may not help you and you may make some wrong decisions in your life which may have a long lasting effect on your career. So apart from the physical body you have to learn to know and manage your mind, also.

Managing the mind is very important for the man to whatever discipline he belongs or to whatever job he does and whatever or whereever he is. Along with free will he is given the Vivek – the capacity to understand what is right and what is wrong. If the man lives as his mind's interest and desires, under the pressure of rag-dwesh of mind then his life no more remains human life. Its life becomes animal life. Therefore man has to manage his mind not by giving order and controlling it but by being its friend. Keep it with you with love by being friendly. Make your mind such a close friend that it will never go away from you. Geeta gives a loud message that mind is our friend and the mind is our enemy also. Don't behave rudely with your mind, but convince it to remain with you, whatever you do, with love and affection and you will experience that you become the real friend of your mind.

The Bhagwan says in the Sixth Adhyaya that to make the mind more concentrated, more contemplative and more equanimous and balanced meditation helps a lot. Bhagwan discusses the whole process of meditation in sixth Adhyaya of Geeta.

First you sit straight on a comfortable seat and control your sense organs and its activities, keep the mind calm and focus it on "ME". – Here during this process an individual has to remember that he is not a single individual but in his mind there are many other individuals, situations and agenda of "To Dos". While meditating these all may disturb the mind. So first unload them all and keep them outside. Always remember no one has the capacity to bother you, unless you allow him to do that. Instead give him freedom to be as he is, accept him as he is and keep your mind free to meditate.

Thus, when you accept all things as they are, your mind will be focussed on Ishwer in meditation. And the meditator gains that state of the mind which is not affected by any mental or outer elemment, just as the Deep burns steadily in a closed room.

If one says that, what Bhagwan says is very difficult and the mind is so active that in between meditation it runs away outside. Bhagwan is very accomodative and says don't worry, let it run away, you go behind it and bring it back lovingly.

Arjuna also asks the same question:

Chanchalam hi manah: Krushna pramathi balvaddradham |
Tasyaham nigraham manye vayoriv sudushkaram ||
(6-34)

The mind is, O Krushna, restless, turbulent, strong and unyielding, I deem it quite as difficult to control as the wind.

Bhagwan shown in many verses of Sixth Adhyaya about meditation and Dhyan Yoga, Arjuna listened attentively but he says the yoga that you discussed does make Seeker's mind steady at times but I do not think, that state of steadiness and focussed mind will continue to be with him all the time. During, Shravan, manan and nididhyasana the mind seems – "SAM" – steady but after that in practice – during the interaction with the world of objects it again becomes unsteady and restless.

Arjuna also says that such calmness and steadiness may be possible as you say but at present, where I am, I don't see any such thing possible for me... as the mind as it is ever turbulent, strong and unyielding.

These three terms used for the mind by Arjuna are quite loaded ones. Turbulance shows not only the speed of the flow of thoughts but also their restlessness and agitations causing stormy waves rising up and down on the surface. The waves of thoughts are not only fast and rough, when reached to its desired objects it gets so powerful and strong that it would become very difficult to pluck the mind away from its attachment. Apart from having turbulent and strong, the third characteristic of mind is that – when, it has reached to its own choice, even for the moment, it becomes "unyielding" and so it is totally impossible for the human being to pull it back from that and persuade it to stay at the chosen point of concentration.

And what an appropriate simile given by Arjuna here "As the wind" that exactly presents the strength and Vigour, the vivacity and treachery and all pervasiveness of the mind! Thus, Arjuna asks the Bhagwan Krushna for some practical ways by which he can gain perfect control over the stormy nature of the "unyielding, strong, turbulent and restless mind."

Arjuna has just experienced that what is the impact of mind! A little while ago he could not even stand on his feet. The whole body was shaking, his dhanush has fallen down from his hand and he has to sit down and declared that he will not fight. His mind went out of his control. So he asks Bhagwan that how can such powerful and turbulent mind can be managed which is as strong as the wind. Apart from all these four qualities of mind one more which makes the simile of mind and wind more relevant is that both are formless. Not visible. How to control that?

To give solace to Arjuna the Bhagwan accepts first Arjuna's arguments and says, yes mind is very difficult to manage but there is a method by which the formless and invincible mind can be brought under control.

The Bhagwan says:

Aashanshaymayan Mahabaho Mano Durnigraham Chalam |
Abhyasen tu Kauntey Vairagyen cha gruhyate ||

O, mighty-armed one, undoubtedly, the mind is difficult to control and is restless, but by practice, O Son of Kunti and by dispassion it is restrained.

Bhagwan Krushna knew his friend Arjuna. He was a great warrior, a man of action, a daring adventurer and had a strong personality. When such a great personality seemed to be shaking, instead of condemning him the Bhagwan approached him with empathy and love. And the real teacher or master always has the balanced mind to decide – how to approach the disciple who is a rebel,who has – intellect with subtle understanding and extreme tact and Bhagwan did that.

The Bhagwan told Arjuna that what you said about the mind is true; There is no doubt in it. But I never say that to control the mind is easy, but I say that by an effort it is also not impossible as what you said about the mind is not its own nature, we made our mind like that. If it was its nature, we can never change it. So do not blame the mind. Mind has become extroverted and turbulent because from the very beginning the man has made the mind as such by letting it be drawn toward the objects of its interest. So it is in fact, not the mind's nature but it is made like that by the man. So man also can divert it into another direction then it would have been different. Therefore nature cannot be changed as fire can not leave its nature – similarly if it happens to be the nature of mind then it can not be controlled at all, but by Abhyas it can be made our friend and quite manageable. So it is not mind's nature so by practice it can be changed.

Bhagwan says, know your mind – If mind rans after the sense objects, then make the Ishwer the object, make the Atman an object – And then the mind will not run after that – Abhyasen.

Another method shown by the Bhagwan is Vairagya – dispassion – mind goes after – RAG – means that object which it likes. Now here the man has to began to see the **'DWESH' (Dosh)** in the RAG after that mind begins to see negative points of RAG – **(Doshdarshan)** – Such an attitude to see Dosh described as **Dosh Darshan.**

Every time the man has to keep this attitude. Then only it will help, How? The man has to think how this object of my likes has brought adverse effect on my body, on my relations, on my name and fame. Remembering this, it will give rise to an attitude to ignore or avoid that object of rag – his intensity of desire for that will go on reducing. Which gave birth to Vairagya. Thus, **Trushna** will be transferred into **Vitrushna** | Here for managing and controlling the mind Bhagwan gives much importance to Abhyas and then show the singnificance of Vairagya too.... and concludes that the mind you can manage not by ordering it but by making a friend by the means of **Abhyas** and **Vairagya.**

Moreover, today's youth – either during study, or during searching for an appropriate job or during a job too, has to face severe competition at every level and so he/she has to run to maintain the place where he/she is. Some problems are faced by today's executives in managing their organisations where they have to fulfil their targets in the deadline given. Consequently life remains full of tension and stress. Of course a certain level of tension and stress are considered essential for maintaining and improving efficiency. But this must remain at a manageable level, otherwise they have to face various stress generated diseases. So to cope with this situation all of them should have a calm and equanimous mind. Such a mind one can have only if one follows what the Bhagwan says about the mind and follow the method shown by Bhagwan.

The manager and our young generation has also to face the pair of opposites like, happiness and sorrow, success and failure, Jay and Parajay, hope and disappointment, frustration etc. If under its pressure they fall apart then they will not be able to find a way to put things again on the right track whenever they happen to face something opposite to their expectations. Everyone should know that in spite of all of his precautions, well-planned effort and excellent performance if he does not achieve the desired result, he should accept that apart from:

Uddhyam, Sahasam, Dhairyum, Buddhim, Shaktim, Parakarmum one needs one more factor and that is Daivam. And this factor plays an important role.

Many factors which are at work in determining the outcome of our endeavour. So invoke the blessings of the Deva through Prayer. In our culture we accept that if in spite of our best effort, if we did not achieve our target; our Karma (Past or Present) is responsible. There are certain specific prayers in Vedas to neutralise our past karma also. Ishwar is karma fal pradata. It is not me that decides the result. So I am not "failure." This attitude of karma yoga works as the shock-absorber and one can accept failure also with balanced mind. Such unique attitude keeps the mind undisturbed and such a mind can tackle the situation skillfully and at times can transfer into a new opportunity for bright future. Therefore the man should concentrate on managing the mind.

Here two guidelines if kept in mind, these helps a lot to manage the situations:

(A) Accept yourself as you are

Accept yourself with all of your strengths and weaknesses. Try to exploit strength and overcome weaknesses with the help of your strong mind which you have made your friend. And be satisfied with yourself. Most of the problems arise as you are not satisfied with yourself. In that case you try to get power, position, wealth, name and fame by thinking that these will make you satisfied and happy. But it will not, in fact you remain continuously under stress and tension to get more and more of it and this will make your mind again disturbed and restless. Instead if you be satisfied with what you are and with what you have, your mind also remainss calm and co-operative. So it is upto you to keep the mind well-managed and then; you will see that you are good and efficient managers, students, teachers or in whatever job you will. Feel comfortly with you.

(B) Accept the world outside as it is

Vedic Vision and the Bhagwan also says that, do not blame the people around or the government, or society or the institutes or your teachers, mentors etc. for your problems or for any of your failures. Accept the situation with the maturity and equanimity of mind – then only with the help of such a mind will you be able to find a way out.

Thus one can never ignore to manage the mind

In whatever field he/she works. If one can manage oneself then only one can manage others by Shamdamadi Qualities which is a part of Sadhan Chatushthaya.

– 13 –

EVERYTHING IS GIVEN

Human beings are self conscious and have self judgement also. The people, especially the youth, are very conscious about how he or she looks. They feel proud and happy if they have a good look, well built body, a costly car or bike and have latest branded clothes etc. They also feel proud for being selected for inter-university cricket match or for having experience in playing football, for passing some competitive examination or for getting a prestigious job immediately after completing the study.

Not only the youth but mankind all over the world has such feelings of "I-ness" and "My-ness". It is me who is so beautiful, so handsome, and so talented. The achivement and success I got is mine. I did it. I achieved this and that. To pass the C. A. exam or to get admission in IIT is not that easy but I got it. Such kind of feeling and thinking is common everywhere irrespective of race, religion or nationality.

Here what is the message that Geeta gives? It may surprise you but it is the fact.

By studying Geeta what one comes to know is the FACT that in this life nothing belongs to ME. Everything that we require in our life is given to us. We are only the visitors in this universe, who came under the Visa for a limited period of time. As visitors our stay here is not permanent. On some fixed day we have to leave. All five Mahabhutas/elements – Earth, Water, Fire, Air and Sky of which our physical body is made are so essential that without which human life is impossible to survive. Earth provides us with food, water; fire and air are also the basic needs of human life. We are indebted to them and so we see Mantras and Stuti of earth, water, vayu, fire, space etc. in Vedas. As these are essential and given free of cost to mankind, it is the responsibility of mankind to take care of these resources and to protect them.

When we came here, we came without bringing anything with us. We were born with a tiny body, having potential for growth but we did not bring with us oxygen, water or food to last for seventy or eighty-ninety years. Nature has kept everything ready for us. It provided plants and trees to take up carbon dioxide and give us oxygen to breath. It seems we have entered a fully furnished guest house.

Thus whatever you find in this universe, you cannot claim your ownership of it. Only the creator, the Ishwer is the owner. You may say, "Okay, I will not claim any other thing of the creation, but what is my creation, say, the business empire that I have built up, have I not ownership of it? "Geeta says, "No". You cannot. For creating a business empire, whatever you need, land, the material to build a building, skill to build a building, furniture, bricks and what not? Did you create all that? Even a small brick is not your creation. It was made of clay. The men have not produced clay. Then on which base can you say it is your creation? It is all given.

Take another example. Suppose of a person, who owns a flat on the third floor of a five storey apartment, she calls that, "This is my flat." But let us examine what she actually owns. She does not own the ground on which the building stands or the floor on which her flat is situated. Even in her own apartment she does not own the floor for it is the ceiling of the fellow down below. She is not even the owner of the ceiling as that is the floor of the person above her. The left wall happens to be the right wall of her neighbour's apartment and the right wall is naturally the left wall of the other neighbour. She cannot say she owns the space inside her walls. She insists that she is the owner but in fact she does not create anything; the contribution of various factors together makes it possible to build a building.

You can say that you have certain things but can never say that you own-these-things. Everything is given to us in this world. Think for a moment what is it that we have created in this world? One of you may say that we have made many inventions but think also that inventions are possible only when there is potential for that is given to the inventors. Going to the moon and return from it was a possible achievement as potentiality to do that was given. But going to and returning from the Sun is not possible. Possibilities of inventions are provided to us by providing that subtle intellect, all the instruments, the skill in producing and using these instruments etc. are given to us. We explorers or researchers only discover what is already there by making the use of all technology along with the skill of invention and using that technology with the help of things given to us.

Let these things keep aside, which are not created by us and are given but may I not say that at least I own my body? One of you may ask this question.

No. no one can claim anything here, not even one's own body. Your mother may say it is mine as I gave birth to you. Your father also may claim it because he was the Nimitta-Karan.* your spouse claims the body belongs to him or her by bond of marriage. Your employer may say as I pay him for his work. I own his body. The state may also claim that as a citizen you have to perform certain duties so it's mine, Even vegetables, wheat, rice etc. can also have their claim on your body because they provide nourishment to it. Similarly the earth will also lay claim on you. Fire can register a claim because it is fire that maintains the temperature of your body as long as you are alive. Water can also be claimed as it maintains the shape of your body. Air that you breathe can also claim you – Still people say, "This is my body".! !

* For creating any thing 3 things are required,

(i)   Material cause– UPADAN KARAN

(ii) Creator – NIMITT KARAN

(iii) Skill to create.

Thus, to make a clay pot we need clay (UPADAN KARAN) pot maker (NIMITT KARAN) and skill to create a pot.

In the case of creation of JAGAT – (the world of objects) UPADAN and NIMITT KARAN is ONE. As we create our dream world where the objects of my dream world and I, the creator are one and the same..Similarly the creation/the world with all its objects including our bodies and Creator/Ishvar is one and the same.

Therefore ownership is only a notion. You do not own your body, or anything outside the body. Even the knowledge you have gained, you received from so many teachers at various levels of your education. You don't even author that. Science, art, languages, mathematics – all this knowledge is given to mankind. The man owes to hundreds and thousands of factors including five mahabhutas for his any kind of achievement. The man owns nothing. He simply lives here and enjoys all kinds of things that are provided or given to him. Therefore the Bhagwan says to Arjuna, "O Arjuna, appreciate everything is my Glory."

Therefore we – Hindus – who are the most cultured people with the oldest civilization appreciate and do Stuti and Pooja of each and every element of nature. We consider the earth as our mother. We have special Stuti and Stotras for Vayu, Fire, Water, Clouds in the Sky. We do give "Arghya " to the Sun every morning by water and chant Gayatri Mantra. We consider River also our mother. The Moon is presented before children as their "Mama" (mother's brother) to create respect to all the natural elements in their mind from Childhood. All are Pujneeya for us. We offer our Puja to the trees, mountains, Sun, Moon, Oceans – everything. It shows the appreciation that I own nothing here. Everything is given to us. So, understand their Value and your duty to protect and appreciate it and show your gratitude to all of them.

But nowadays under the wrong imitation of western culture and under Macolle's education policy under British rule our young generation forgot our great heritage. If we would have continue to follow that tradition there would not have been problems of polluted air, polluted water, misuse of earth and their consequent natural calamities – But instead we continue to throw poisonous gas of factories into the air, industrial waste is dumped into the sea, dirty water is thrown into our rivers, we also take everything from the earth – water, oil, gas, different hints of ores and build high buildings and hotels on the slopes of Himalayan mountain. All nature has provided in enough amounts and in its pure form to us but we – created chaos, disturbed nature and polluted everything. When we enter into any well furnished guest house for a limited period of time, its owner expects us to leave it as it was. And if we have caused any harm to its furniture etc. we have to pay its cost. Similarly here nature punishes mankind for its wrongdoing in the form of natural calamities, like floods, landslides, famine, earthquake and what not? But still under the pressure of his interest man's behaviour remains irresponsible.

Therefore the young generation has to accept that they own nothing. Everything is given. Bhagwan says in Tenth Adhyaya, that whatever talent you see anywhere in any person is mine. Every glory you see on this earth is mine. Because I am the material cause of the whole creation and cause of Jagat. The wind that blows is myself, the Sun that shines is myself. I am the wisdom of the wise. The sweet voice of the singer is a gift from me. That Eyes can see is my glory that ears can hear is my glory. Wherever there is some extra ordinary glory, you must see me there. Although I am everywhere but see me particularly in these special things where I shine more. Among all the mountains, I am the Himalayas. Among the peaks I am the Everest. Among the rivers I am the Ganga. There is no special power that belongs to anyone else. All fame, all power, all kinds of glory belongs to me only. Thus, no one can claim anything here, not even his own body on which many have their claim. Thus, Bhagwan says that ownership is only a notion. Everything is given to you here.

Therefore He says to Arjuna and all of our youngsters who are today's Arjunas to appreciate all as my glories. Whatever is glorious, prosperous, powerful full of strenth know it to be but spark of my glory. So, in this way Bhagwan very wonderfully describes all the glories of His own, and says Arjuna, to appreciate His glories in everything. So, man should not have (AHANKAR) arrogance for anything which he has, but consider it His grace, His glory and appreciate the Ishwar and all the nature for whatever they have and whatever they are. As nature has given so many things to mankind, then it is the responsibility of the man to appreciate all and take care of environment to keep it pollution-free and pure for generations to come.

14

VALUE IN BUSINESS: A CRUX FOR MANAGEMENT SCENARIO

(BHARTIYA VISION)

INTRODUCTION:

At the entrance of the central hall of the Parliament House, where the constitution 'of India was debated and approved, the following words from Bhartruhari's "NEETISHATAKAM" are inscribed:

"AYAM NIJO PARO VETI GANANA LAGHUCHETSA |
UDAR CHARITANA TU VASUDHAIV
KUTUMBAKAM | |"

The meaning is:

This is mine that is yours; this is the concept of small minds. But to those who have a higher consciousness, the whole world is family.

From that ideal state where the whole world is considered as family in India, we have now come to a stage where the whole world is described as a 'MARKET'. The journey of being a member of one family to becoming a competitor in a market is a tragedy of our times.

Here books like "The Final Exit" (Derek Hamfree) in U.S., "The Complete Manual of committing Suicide" in Japan, "The Suicides users' Manual" in France became the 'best seller books'. According to the UNESCO Report, 54 percent of death of young people in the U.S., Sweden and Japan is due to suicide and 44 percent of executives falling under the age-group of 40 to 45 are mentally diseased.

This is the present scenario. This shows that people need some teaching in spiritual matters, values etc. in personal as well as as business life. Is there a way out? Yes. Even in the midst of the global competitive market's materialism, we have a hope – in the teaching of our scriptures.

Present Scenario:

In the 21st century the business environment has undergone revolutionary changes. The ups & downs of the economies, the changing desires and attitudes of customers and governments, rapidly advancing technology, inflated cost of energy, material, and labour, awareness towards environment protection, consumer safety, changing political scenario, development of competitive global market etc. have influenced the organization and management intensively.

It was not that people did not think over values in business during the 19th and in 20th century. But the way of thinking was quite different till 1980's. We saw three different phases of development in the area of management responsibility which is a long time duration of about 200 years.

Phase one was of the value of profit maximisation management where the only value was, "what is good for me (self interest) is good for my country."

Phase two was of the value of Trusteeship management when control went into the hands of paid professionals, the value became, "what is good for my business is good for my country."

Phase three was of the value of quality of life management where the value became, "what is good for the society is good for my business."

This development took place in developed countries. As far as India is concerned, our culture and civilisation, which is one of the oldest civilisations, the whole society is value based from the vedic times.

What is value?

The term VALUE generally indicates the regard for a thing, situation or attitude which for some reason is esteemed or prized by the value holder. In Sanskrit an ethical value is defined as 'DHARMA', a standard or norm of conduct derived from the way which I wish others to behave with me. What I expect or want from others becomes my standard/norm or DHARMA. i.e. right behaviour and what I do not want others to do is "A-DHARMA", i.e. wrong behaviour. This is equally true in determining the norms of behaviour among different business enterprises and among different countries in the use of natural resources, protection of environment, safety of customers, expectations and hopes of people at large etc. These values including the age-old values of non-injury, honesty, humility, charitableness, truthfulness etc. are not just arbitrary man-made rules but they emerged from the inherent common regard for one's own interest, comfort and conflict-free life. These are natural and universal and known to all. The values do not need any education. There may be some cultural variation in degree or in emphasis among different countries but basic values and norms do have certain universality. Moreover, these values are not absolute. These are relative. There may be situations where what is considered ethical becomes unethical depending upon certain context. But these are never purely subjective. Thus, although relative sometimes in applicability, basic values have a universal content. This consensus is not negated by the fact that these values may be subject to interpretation in some situations – i.e. in war the value of non-injury is kept suspended but it is situational and does not affect the basic value. In brief, values are universal in content but relative and situational in their applicability. This basic truth should be followed by management in today's global market, if it wants to keep the world safe for future generations.

Indian philosophy tells us to always remember one thing that you – as an individual, as an organisation and as a country not only a consumer but a contributor and the role of CONTRIBUTOR is more important than that of CONSUMER. Contributor's role implies along with some contribution a care, discrimination (VIVEK) and maturity in making use of natural resources, human resources and the environment as a whole. Such an attitude and understanding makes the world nice and safe to live in.

Base of Indian Ethos:

Indian Ethos has their roots in these values which in turn are derived from our Vedic scriptures. These are the source of strength which sustained the Indian civilization and made it survive over 6000 years despite many onslaughts of History. Greece, Roman and Egyptian culture are gone with their Gods and Goddesses. While in India, even today the same old hymns are chanted with the same tune in which they were chanted thousands years ago. Indian Ethos with some eternal values helps this great Indian culture to survive. Indian ethos is drawn from the Vedas, the Upnishads, the Bhagvadgita, the Ramayana and Mahabharat. Indians were used to managing their trade and industry according to these values. Management was not new to Indians. In production and trade India was almost the leading country in the world. The Shantiparva of Mahabharat and Kautilaya's Arthshastra discussed the management of state in detail.

Some of these Ethos are discussed here in this book:

(1) Unique concept of Karma (Action/Work)

Every Karma/work is viewed as DUTY and it is the only means to grow and to develop-available to human beings. The purpose of work is to manifest whatever skill, talent, intelligence and experience one has with oneself. Thus, work is a privilege of living human beings; only dead-bodies are non-working. Hence, KARMA is natural and it is not taken as a burden. It is a duty to be performed in a given situation. work performed with such a mindset is always pleasant. Mind remains calm and at peace. Further one has not to find joy and pleasure outside one's work, because action/Karma performed considering it as DUTY, with full vigour, interest, concentration and enthusiasm itself becomes a great source of joy. This is something unique.

Further every Karma is important in its place. No work is either superior or inferior. The fact is that we have different kinds of jobs to achieve some common goals. Therefore the saying, "I don't want to be a cog in the wheel but I want to be a node" is wrong in our view. Even to be a cog is fine. We consider the bolt as important as the piston. Suppose the piston says to nuts and bolts that I only work and you are not doing anything and if it continues to tease nuts and bolts and if they in response try to move and move and move, what happens to the piston? Therefore, every work or job is equally important like any other job.

(2) Unique attitude towards KARMA/work:

Not only Karma. is considered DUTY and means of one's growth and development, but is also a means to manifest whatever capabilities, one has, i.e. one's divinity within and it is the Ishwar,who has given the energy, skill, ability to work, intelligence, opportunity and everything to enable one to perform any action. Hence, every work has to be pure, good, honest, sincere and appropriate.

Moreover, Karma is always related to its RESULT. And the RESULT may not be exactly what you wanted. It may be more, less, equal or opposite than what you wanted. Our scriptures say that a man is having a privilege of "free choice". He can select to act, non to act or to act differently. Thus he has freedom here and also control over his action. But so far as result is concerned he should know that this falls under the jurisdiction of LAWs or NATURE and he does not know all the laws which contribute to the result, but he does know that THINGS function very systematically and in an organised manner in this universe according to these laws, on which he has no control. He dedicated his work at the altar of God, the result will naturally come from HIM only and so he accepts it as 'PRASAD'. Gratitude – such an attitude helps him to accept the result – whatever it may be with an open mind without apprehensions, just as you accept PRASAD in any temple.

This unique attitude works as a shock absorber. Others fall apart when they meet with failure but the Indian way of viewing the FACT does not allow even a thought of defeat or frustration, when the result is quite the opposite. While our executives can take it with a balanced mind. He knows that the saying, "An executive is paid to show the results, not to give excuses" does not work in the present scenario as the whole business life is full of hidden variables and here this healthy attitude is required.

But one should not worry. Lord Krishna says in GITA, "your freedom, your right is in the performance of action; you keep performing action and let me worry about the result. I will take care of the results."

This may sound frustrating as generally it is believed that the man is not motivated to work unless he gets some benefits as a result of it. But our scriptures say that man has to perform action wherever he is. He cannot escape action. Action or work is the only means available to him for development, evolution for growth, for gaining happiness or anything that he desires to achieve in his life. But he must learn, what he is required to do, how to do it and what is the real purpose of action. This is KARMA YOGA.

(3) KARMA YOGA – A crux for intelligent living:

KARMYOG is defined from two points of view in GITA. From the point of view of KARMA it is "YOGA KARMASU KAUSHALAM." And from the point of view of the result of Karmafal it is SAMAYAM YOGA UCHYATE". How? Only human beings are given free will. They can choose. For this we have some norms or standards on the basis of which we can choose to act, not to act or act in a different way. We are given the discretion (VIVEK) for choosing any action. Thus the base of choosing is value/ DHARM i.e. right thing to be done in given situation. The knowledge of which is in-built in every human being. Thus only skill in action in its literal sense is not Karma-Yoga. If it is so then the thief or terrorist who has skill in his job will also be a Karmyogi. But it is not so.

And this is very important in personal as well as business life. Values do play an important role in making use of free will. A question is raised sometimes: Can we safely dismiss a concern for values in the business world? The answer our culture gives is 'NO'. We cannot escape from values because no one living in this world can escape a relationship based upon his concern that he may not be hurt, cheated, exploited or disturbed. And every society has its own culture, values and ethical norms which are supposed to be observed by the members of the society in their own interest. Hence, they cannot be an exception. This is skill in action.

While performing action one should remember that the past is dead, future is not yet born, hence concentration on present can only bring out excellence in performance. Then only he can develop the ability to accept the result – whatever it may be – with perfect equilibrium of mind, showing emotional maturity. This will make possible a deeper introspection which enable one to see clearly where the things went wrong and why? Here one becomes the master of all situations and never be a victim of the same. Here one is objective and understands the reality. If the cup is half empty, it is half empty. Then only he is said to have a healthy attitude and right vision that is very much needed to face challenges of hidden variables in the era of globalisation.

(4) The SELF (ATMAN) is the source of all power.
(Atmana Vidhyate Viryam) Kenopanishad 2: 4

Every human being has the same Atman. A human being is just not a physical body with some skill. Within this body, there lies the Atman which is the same in everyone. Every human being has the same **Atman** with immense potentiality to grow and develop within. Therefore the management has to treat them accordingly. It is management's responsibility to bring out this divinity from the employees. Vedant's Karma Yoga helps them to bring "The God in Man" and shows them how to manifest their inner divinity in their work and behaviour.

Thus, in Indian Philosophy motivation is internal and not external. Bhagavad Gita is a story of motivation. Arjuna has lost his motivation due to some obstacles, wrong thinking and confusion in his mind. All that is required is the removal of all these.

But how can we do this? How can we turn managers into Karma-Yogi? Is it possible in today's environment? Yes, it is possible. If Lord Krishna could turn Arjuna in to a Karma-Yogi in the battlefield itself and if Mahatma Gandhi could turn Indian youth into Karma-Yogi during freedom movement which made them to dedicate their lives to the cause of freedom without attachment i.e. without thinking about the result, then there is no doubt that it is possible for the management to turn its employees into 'Karma-Yogis even in this ever-changing world.

(5) Welfare of All YAGNA-BHAVNA
(Nih Shreyas and Abhyuday)

Management in developed countries emphasis on profit and productivity. Their major goal is to obtain material success and major share in the global market. Moral and ethical values have secondary place in business. Even P. F. Drucker rejected the idea that business can run on ethics and values in 1985.

In the Indian way of management also material success, profit and large market share, no doubt are considered important but profit is not the major goal. Vedanta teaches to perform all the activities 'Atmano Mokshartham, Jagat Hitaya Cha". Serve your personal interest but do not forget others' interest. SANKARACHARYA has given the concept of "NIH SHREYAS" and "ABHYUDAYA", which brings perfection in individual life along with the welfare of the society, nation and the whole world.

In western world a change has taken place since 1988. Kenneth Blenchard and Vincent Peale wrote a book, "The power of Ethical management" (William Marrow and Camp, New-York). On the cover of this book was written the line, "Integrity pays, you don't have to cheat to win". At another place a sub-title was found, "Managing only for profit is like playing tennis with your eye on the scoreboard and not on the ball" In Japan also business ethics have been developed which can be seen in ZEN teaching.

We do have this thinking from the Vedic age. The Lord Krishna says in GITA, chapter 3, stanza 13, that all the sorrows from the society would be removed if socially conscious members of a community feel satisfaction in enjoying the "REMNANTS" of their work, performed in the YAGNA-SPIRIT. He added, "Those who cook for themselve are criminals." What an enlightened idea expressed thousands of years ago!

That is why a lesson is given in our culture, "Do your work, consider it your duty, earn according to your ability and skill, spend a part of your earnings for the welfare of others and always follow a path of DHARMA or values." Gandhiji's trusteeship concept has also emerged from this basic concept of Yagna spirit. The chapter on Kapil-Devhuti Samvad in Bhagavatam also describes more clearly the concept of the worship of God in human beings. We respect not only human beings but also all the living beings on earth. All that is here is nothing but the manifestation of Ishvar and therefore we do love care and protect all that is here. This is the unique way of thinking or our scriptures.

Today science has also shifted from the NEWTONIAN I-THOU fragmented dualistic world view to this HOLISTIC world view emerging out of Heisenberg's uncertainty principle, the latest discoveries in Quantum Physics and the successful experimentations of Bell's Theorem, which has much similarity in our holistic vision of Vedanta Philosophy.

(6) Means Are Equally Important As The Ends.

(YADRISI BHAVANA YASYA SIDDHI BHAVATI TADRISI")

Means are given equal importance in our culture. Objectives of any organisation must not only be in correspondence to the Values prevailing in the society, the means applied for achieving these objectives must also be pure, just, honest and non-harming.

We find around us much dishonesty and corruption and we also see such people wealthy and seemingly happy. This may create a doubt in our youth about the Values. But we know that they also pay the cost of following A-DHARM. Such people do not have mental peace or happiness within. They generally suffer from several stress generated diseases. They remain restless, agitated and empty inside. And at sometime in their life they do find that money or wealth can not buy health, happiness or mental peace.

In fact nobody likes dishonesty, corruption or falsehood. Even the greatest cheater does not like to be cheated by others. Thus dishonest corrupt people also expect honesty from others. Similarly everyone loves kindness, honesty and to be loved. This shows that we have values for all these things in the core of our heart. This is our nature. Gandhiji has applied this in practice.

Hence even in the times of globalisation, management is required to observe purity in means to be applied and they will definitely gain respect, loyalty, initiative and enthusiasm of all the persons working with them all over the world as people still have respect and love for these basic values which are universal in nature.

(7) Sharing Material Prosperity and Spiritual Achievements with Others.

Any business organisation is considered as sound as its management of human resources. Management of people is not that easy. A large number of theories and concepts have been developed in western management philosophy in this area. We also do have some such concepts from the Vedic age. Meaning of such MANTRA is as under:

Common be our PRAYERS.

Common be our ENDS.

Common be our PURPOSE.

Common be our DELIBERATIONS.

Common be our DESIRES.

United be our HEARTS.

United be our INTENTIONS.

Perfect be the union amongst us.

Now-a-days we are talking about many things like prayers in the morning in corporations, management by objectives, involving people in determining objectives, taking interest in employees' personal life etc. All these elements are in the above MANTRAS from the Vedic age, following of which problems can be minimised and productivity can be maximised. We also do have another important MANTRA leading to cordial relations with the employees.

OM SAHANA VAVATU

SAHANAU BHUNAKTU

SAHVIRYAM KARVA VAHAI

TEJASWINA VADHITAMASTU

MA VIDVISHAVAHAI

OM SHANTI, SHANTI, SHANTIHI

Om may the Almighty protect us both. (The teacher and the disciple, the manager and subordinates) May He nourish us both. May we work together with great energy. May study (Keeping pace with advancing knowledge in respective areas) be vigorous and fruitful. May we not hate/quarrel with each other. Om, Peace, I Peace, Peace.

In ancient India every activity including business activity was based on such concepts given in our scriptures – like YAJNA SPIRIT which implies sacrificing individual interest in favour of larger benefits of others, SREYAS, which implies preferring long term benefits over short term gains and SHARING which implies sharing prosperity, earning and everything with others. In Indian culture business organisation is viewed not as a means of profit making but for the overall development and growth – physical, intellectual and spiritual – of individuals, organisations and the whole mankind towards its perfection.

(8) Macro Vision:

Most suffer from micro vision and self centred views of life. Instead of this we are required to macro vision as taught in VEDANTA where it is stated that I am not a single solitary individual but I am a part of the whole universe.

All of us are interrelated with each other and each of us has certain roles to play, certain responsibilities to exercise towards the society.

Developing such macro vision is the need of today's world. Globalisation has made the world a "small village". All the nations are woven into one fabric. An event that takes place in one corner can affect the whole world. Hence management has to learn to view the problems and situations on a bigger canvas by coming out of its micro vision and keeping in view the welfare of the whole mankind while taking any management decision.

We have in our VEDANTA such macro vision due to which Indian culture and civilisation have survived as precious as ever. The great management thinkers of the western world including some of the great scientists have also accepted the oneness of the whole universe now.

Thus, this Indian Ethos have the strength to turn the whole scenario inside out.

A question may arise here in the mind of the youth that in spite of having such great ancient heritage, why do we see all around in India, decline and fall of these values? The nation which has a very rich culture and values and which has drawn the attention of other countries in the early times and even today, why does it itself suffers so many sproblems?

This may be due to wrong interpretation of the values and concepts of our Indian culture by some vested interests in our own country – like determination of caste by birth, (In fact our scriptures state that a caste depends on GUNAs and qualities – inborn and acquired) blind and mindless pursuit of rituals etc. These vested interests wanted to have all power in their hands by denying education and access to knowledge to the majority of people. Women, traders and workers became their victims. Manual labour started to be considered as the lowest form of work, (while our scriptures consider every work as sacred and important in its place and accept the dignity of labour). Consequently a guilt complex and inequity started to prevail in society. Thus, lessons taught by our Vedas, Upnishada and Bhagvadgita were interpreted wrongly and the whole society has gradually become divided.

The Britishers saw the divided India and destroyed whatever good was left. They associated Indian Ethos and values wrongly with so many inhumane practices like untouchability, caste-system based on birth, wasteful Vedic rituals etc.

Moreover, Indians who got education through English in British schools and colleges and taught distorted history of our country also become the victims of this prejudice. They also lost respect for their own national heritage, culture values etc. This is the reason why a Hindu is not having any knowledge and respect for his Hindu Dharma which a Christian and Muslim does have. A Muslim or Chrisitan is always proud about his being a Muslim or Christian and has respect for his religion, while a Hindu (The majority of India) who has taken education in English medium institutions managed by FATHERS and NUNS has neither knowledge of his Hindu Religion nor any respect for the same. Such so-called liberalised Hindus have no knowledge of Indian Ethos, (derived from Vedic/Hindu scriptures) values etc. And still a systematic effort to destroy our culture and heritage is being carried out by very well globally organised and very well financed (from outside) powerful organisations. Therefore, our youth should be very alert to protect our ancient culture.

In such scenario it is very important to remember that according to ancient Vedic scriptures, business organisations is created by the society as an instrument of not only wealth but also welfare and well being of the people to attain socially desirable goals (not the goals desired by the society) through ethically worthy means, resulting in generation of healthy – physically, mentally and spiritually – wholesome individuals who carry ethical values and positive impulses into their community leading towards the welfare and well being of the whole nation.

The above is possible if we follow Indian Ethos and values in business management. In fact, we should be very proud of having such values and such unique vision to view the THINGS. Ours' is a holistic vision and unless some such vision is applied in management when the whole world has become a 'global village', it would not be possible for the business world to face today's challenges within and without successfully. Moreover, only such a vision can help to keep the world SAFE for the future generations.Now it is the responsibility of the youth to make it happen.

15

ROLE OF THE EXECUTIVE

(Lesson Learned From Geeta)

It is said generally, "An executive is paid to show the results, not to give excuses."

No doubt, one works for the result. But in the present business scenario, for this, an executive can not be less than God. But even God goes by rules. He also has to say sometimes, "Hey, I am sorry. I have to follow the law of Karma. So I cannot do anything more." Thus, even God has to give excuses and say, "I have to go on the base of your Karma. I cannot give you more than I am giving you now." So even God can not be the executive who will get things done as management wants, always.

Therefore one should have a certain healthy attitude to view things. One should accept certain realities. The problem arises when the expected result does not come as there are many hidden variables which are uncontrollable. In this world what we have not expected will happen and what one expected does not happen. The whole life of a man is full of uncertainties. What does a poor executive do?

Our Vedic scriptures have a certain vision which says that the man is given a free will. It is his jurisdiction but after selecting the work, the result will come as par the laws of nature, over which the man has no control.

Now, think, do people plan to get admitted in the ICU of a hospital? But the ICU ward remains full. This conveys a very significant truth in our lives. Something occurs that you have not expected in spite of all your efforts. This is the fact that you have to accept and for this you need that healthy attitude of Vedic vision that you offer your every Karma to the Ishvar and take the result as the prasad from the Ishvar. If you understand this, you won't have a breakdown in adverse situations. Then you have enough space inside that allows you to take the situations as they are and you can find some solution with equanimity of mind.

Otherwise what happens when the executive see that result is quite opposite to his expectation, he starts considering himself a 'loser'. But here you should remember that every loss there is certain gain. It gives a useful lesson to be learned. Even in small small things we are helpless, suppose, I ask you, "what would be your next thought? Tell me." Nobody knows. That means what? That means you are helpless. Now I request you to be angry for a minute. You can not do that even. Thus, your limitations are many. There are limitations in terms of your knowledge, power, resources, time, place etc. But on the other hand you can also say that you have achieved many successes in your life against every odd and gain the position and status in an organisation.

Thus, you are not a 'loser'. In fact, you are on the driver's seat. And when you are in the driver's seat, you should be ready for the potholes and pitfalls. The driver's seat is not that easy or comfortable but it is good to feel that you are in charge and you can manage the situation in your own way.

Now, another thing is – you can either say, "My cup is half empty" or "My cup is half full." Both describe the fact. But attitude is different which depends upon one's understanding of certain realities.

It is a fact that we have various desires, and having desires is not a problem. It is the endowment from Ishvar to mankind alone. Bhagwan says in Geeta, "Dharma – Avivuddh Kamosmi." But these desires are to be satisfied by using the right means.

Remember, the whole life is a percentage of a game. Either you succeed in getting what you desire or may have to face failure. So be ready for any surprise, which may come according to the hidden variables – including your own past Karma. Therefore, if I meet with failure, I will say, "It is my Karma." Now this attitude is a shock-absorber. In other cultures they fall apart when they meet with failure but in our specific vision helps us to stay safe. Because we have a theory that our past Karma – in this birth and in any other innumerable past births frutify and unfold everyday. In other cultures, the word 'luck' is used which means that which occurs without having any cause. 'Luck' is something that does not have any cause. It is an unexpected experience. Here it comes as per law of nature. It is like swimming. If you swim along with the current, the speed of river water becomes a 'Plus' Point for you but when you swim against the current river water, efforts are to be more and result may be less or nil.

Every executive should know this. When I take all Precautions, Plan well, do well and then even I don't find result I have to accept that there are certain hidden variables. As from Bhagwan we learn in Geeta, we can absorb the shock by thinking of our Past Karma and also can pray for taking care of such hidden variables. We have prayers in Vedas for facing unpredictable and unexpected situations – general and specific. – Prayer is a Karma and therefore it has its falam (result). So they neutralize the effect of those forces and provide us mental peace to face the situation effectively. Thus, we don't say, "our good luck" or "our bad luck." But we say, "It is our Karma" by believing that our past Karma – good and bad follow us and unfold everyday, affecting our efforts positively or negatively.

Thus, (Daivam) – fate is something that is there and one should not be afraid of it, because that is the game of Percentage. So when you plan, plan in the best possible way and then work hard to win. Never think that I may lose. Never have fear of failure, but prepare to face courageously – what comes. Then only you will have calm mind to find out a way to minimise the loss and put the organisation again on the right track

TEAM BUILDING:

For today's executive his team and its spirit contributes a lot. As an executive you have to provide leadership and take the team with you. It is not easy to make people work for you. And why should anyone work for you? It is said often that an employee works for money, not for his leader. Even after getting a good job, people continue to see "Wanted" columns in newspapers. They always look for a better job. So an executive is required to keep his employees interested in his present job.

Executive must remember that a human being is a human being. He wants certain involvement, certain care and consideration from the management. He wants the executive to treat him as his equal. In position he may not be equal, but as a human being, he is equal. He does not like to be bossed. While working in a team under any executive in any project he would like to be involved in the project. So an executive has to make every member of the team feel equally important and to see that he gets an opportunity to contribute his idea, his creativity to the Project.

Moreover, in building up the team-spirit communication also plays a great role. Everything should be reached clearly and exactly to everyone in the team. There should not be any, "Verbal-Entropy". Entropy means in the process of reaching the message something has changed.

Therefore communication has to be brief and clear. Our Scriptures says, it should be in Alpaksharam, (minimum words), Asandigdham (unambiguous), Akshobhyam (grammatically proper), Anpadhyam (not in contrast with) what is said earlier. Everything related to the project is to be conveyed clearly upto the last person. It is also essential to establish the method of communication. Which makes the message to reach the last man in his own language and with its clear translation. Here entropy is possible. So executives should remain vigilant for that.

In a team no one is inferior or superior. They have only to perform different jobs. There is a saying in western countries, "I don't want to be a cog in the wheel but I want to be a node." This kind of thinking is wrong. The cog is equally important like the node or piston. Suppose a piston says to the nuts and bolts that I am only working and you both are doing nothing and if it continues to tease nuts and bolts and in anger if they both try to move, and move and move, what will happen to the piston? Therefore remember, every person, every job is equally important in any organization set up.

Providing leadership:

As an executive you are the leader of your men, you should create such an environment in your team that your people feel free to tell you everything. Suppose an employee writes you a letter stating, 'I am suffering from fever and so I want a day's leave." In fact this was not true. Fact is that his uncle came from the village and wanted to take him to Tirupati Balaji Temple for Darshan. Now the question is why should he tell a bluff? For this you as an executive and as a leader are responsible. Think, if he would have told you the truth, you might have not allowed him to go there. This is the problem. In this way executives create bluffers out of people who are originally plain, simple, honest and sincere. Instead, you as an executive should make them feel free to tell you the truth and make them feel big, important and inspire them to present their creative ideas about the project on which they work.

Leadership can be provided more efficiently by the help of proper communication, proper empowerment, proper behavior and interaction of the leader with his men in the organisation.

We know communication is a two-way traffic. But the organisational hierarchy is too long to have a direct dialogue or contact. But at every level the immediate head/boss should give people under him a sense of being understood. Then only communication can be complete and effective. Remember always, how Bhagwan Shri Krushna listened to Arjuna very patiently without interrupting him in between. Similarly, you also have to be a good listener.

Even If you know well, about what he/she is going to tell you, you should listen peacefully without interrupting him in between. You should make him feel fully understood. This person then will work for you with full dedication and commitment. Here in listening, you need not agree with what that person told you, why you do this or that also you can explain him later on, if need arises. This is the way to be a good executive and a leader – not only this but such an attitude will help you to be a good father, good husband/wife, son or daughter or even a good human being.

Perfectionalism And Empowerment:

In providing effective leadership the executive should give proper attention to empowerment. Many people have a sense of perfectionalism. They want everything perfect. This only means the fear of failure and fear of things going wrong. Such people hesitate to delegate authority. They insist on perfection in everything and so fail to empower the people under him. Whenever you delegate or empower, you have to make some compromise but as a perfectionalist you are afraid to do so. You do not have trust that others also can perform that job as you would have done.

Here our unique vision says – you should not worry. As all that is here in the universe is in perfect order of all kinds – like Psychological order, biological order, Physiological order, Cosmopolic order etc. So ours is a perfect world because of its orders. Thus, when all things are in order why should you feel things have to be perfect? Nothing is imperfect here. The fact is you can do any work or job rightly or you do it wrongly. So as an executive it is true for you also. You may also make mistakes, so you should accept others' mistakes too. Thus, trust in MEN plays an important role in delegation and empowerment. So the executives must have trust in his team members. If you cannot, then there arise many problems.

So, better you begin to trust others and delegate some jobs to them and empower them for that. You may also first follow the policy of fake it and make it. It means even if you don't have trust, you act and respond as though you have full trust in them. And you see, it will work. That is Psychological order. Your men will feel that our Head has placed trust in us and so now it is our duty to prove it. And thus they become trustworthy. Just as by swimming you can learn to swim, by singing you can learn to sing, by delegating you learn how to delegate, when and to whom to delegate.

All that I am talking about is from my study of Upanishads, Geeta and our scriptures from my teachers. These books do not tell those things directly but when we have true vision, such thinking arises in our mind which helps us to solve the problems we face in our personal and professional life.

Postponement of Decision Making:

Postponement in decision making is also a very crucial decision in the current business scenario. It also implies Priority management – what is to be done now, what later on and what is to be postponed.

Postponement is a deliberate decision. When and why the executive takes a decision to postpone? It may be because of any reason in life – one is not in that mood, One feels tired, or one thinks that he is not fully prepared. This is wise postponement. Otherwise the decision taken in that situation might prove wrong or have adverse effects in the long run.

All of us have to postpone our decisions for want of enough data, want of the right frame of mind, want of time, want of other resources etc. This kind of postponement due to such causes is quite reasonable. Nothing wrong with it.

But there is also another kind of postponement. It is known as, "Procrastination." It is shown in Bhagavad Geeta as Deerghsutri. It comes from a certain psychological frame of mind. Here one takes too much time in doing assigned work, seems always busy, but at the end he does not succeed to materialise the targets given. Some people make it their policy. A few politicians also believe that some important national problems can be solved only by procrastination. They make a show that they are doing many things, but in fact they do not contribute anything concrete. Such an attitude is totally wrong. That can create problems even in their daily personal life if they continue to be Deerghsutri. Relationships may be broken. Suicidal tendency may be seen leading broken personal bonds.

Therefore no one can afford to procrastinate. So the executive must insist on doing work within the given deadline and never accept delays under any excuse. If there are files to attend, attend to them right now, never let the things go losing.

Behaviour of an Executive:

This also plays a big role. Executive's behavior should be healthy, fair and appropriate. As an executive you need to tell your people about many things, say what you want, what you feel, but let it be Priyam and Hitam. Even the most pleasant thing can be made unpleasant by the way you say it. Vada tells, "Vaang me Madhumattama

". Let there be honey on my tongue. Whatever he tells his people must come from within his heart and his men must feel that. He must also have the value of spoken words. Words can motivate but they can hurt also if not properly used. That hurt may remain for a whole lifetime. Executive must understand the value of speaking pleasantly. Then even if necessary the most unpleasant thing can also be said in an appropriate way. At the same time he should also ensure that his dignity and self-respect is not eroded by others. It is also equally important.

Moreover people should feel free to come to you and talk to you without any fear. If your staff is afraid of you, you are not a proper executive. It does not mean that you should keep the doors of your chamber always open for anyone at any time. But he should make such an environment that if someone needs to come and talk to you he/she must feel free to do that without any fear. Thus, an executive is required to have that skill to create an environment by his behaviour and interaction with the people without losing his own dignity and respect.

Doing Difficult Job – First:

In decision making also an executive is to be ready to take the right decision at the right time. So never put off unpleasant decisions. Make them right now. At times, procrastination in decisions may cause many problems. Nowadays we see the present government of India followed and took it as a habit from the very beginning of its coming into power of doing difficult jobs first. It disposes off column 370 from Jammu and Kashmir very fast and in time. Thus, it is advisable to dispose of difficult decisions first and then make the decisions which are easy or less problematic later. You can start doing this right now and you will find yourself a different person. Fake it and make it.

Finally I would love to quote a beautiful Sanskrit Verse which I always do whenever I go to deliver a lecture in any Management Seminar or Conference. The verse explains the qualities which ensure success, be it personal or professional life as any family head or corporate head.

Udyamam Sahasam, Dhairyam, Buddhi Shakti, Parakramam |
Shadeth Yatra Vartante Tatra Devah Sahaykrut ||

It is said in this verse that the person, who is hard working, who is ready to take calculated risk, who can maintain patience in critical situations, who has an intellectual approach towards everything. Who has skill and ability to acquire essential resources, who has a skill to read and understand the hidden variables in competitive global markets, has potential to get success. And whoever is having these six qualities he is helped by **Daivam –** by divine force/Ishwar.

Thus, with these Six Qualities, if one involves the Ishwar by prayer to take care of hidden variables, he gets success. According to our culture and traditions, we believe that if our own past deeds are against us, "Adrasht Falam" of prayer will neutralise the expected adverse result of any project and if our luck/our good trust deeds are with us, it can enhance our result/our profit from every project. And if it is so, it is a crucial point to be considered by involving Ishwar through prayer by the executive. And nothing is wrong in it, as it is not going to cause even any harm!

What is an idea?

APPENDIX – 1

VARNA VYAVASTHA
(CHATURVARNA)

The Bhagwan says, I have created the Varna-Vyavastha on the basis of Guna and Karma. In Spite of being its creator (Karta) you know me – immutable (Parmeshwar) as A-Karta.

**Chaturvarnyam Maya Srushtam
Gunkarmvibhagyoho |
Tasya Kartarahampi Mam Viddhi
Akartaram Avyayam | | (13-4)**

What is Varnashram Vyavstha? Bhagwan says, this fourfold – Varna (Caste) has been created by me according to the differentiation of GUNA and KARMA, though I am the author there of, know me non-doer and immutable.

Here the word, "Varna " is used to show the different shades of texture or colour in the Yogic sense. In Yoga Shastra, they attribute some definite colour for the three Gunas of which the mind is constituted. Thus, Sattwa is considered white which indicates Purity, calmness and satwikata of mind. Rajas as red which indicates activities making the mind agitated and restless, and Tamas as black indicating idle and lethargic mind – Thus, on base of such Psychological division of mind this Varna Vyavastha is created.

As the mind is made of three Gunas – sattva, rajas and tamas, we see the different combination of these three Gunas differently in every human mind. So our Shastra classified mankind into four Varnas. Just we divide people by profession as doctors, advocates, judges, professors, students, traders, farmers, workers, politicians etc. So too on the basis of mental composition or different textures of mind, the four Varnas are created. Remember that it is according to the differentiation of the composition of mind and the mind is Chaturvidh and it has three Gunas.

Every mind is made of these three Gunas – Sattva, rajas and tamas. But the combination of these three Gunas is different in every mind, which can be divided in four ways:

1. Sattwa – Rajas – Tamas (Means sattwa is predominant, then comes rajas and tamas)

2. Rajas–Sattwa–Tamas (Here Rajas is on the top)

3. Rajas-Tamas-Sattwa (Here also Rajas is on the top)

4. Tamas – Rajas – Sattva – (Here Tamas predominates)

Thus, four combinations are named as (1) Brahman, (2) Kshatriya, (3) Vaishya and (4) Shudra.

Bhasyakar says the mind in which Sattwa Predominates is of Brahmana Varna. This mind is introvert, loves knowledge and Shama, Dama, Tapas,

Purity, Swaddyaya, Shraddha in Ishwar, compassion, Kshama etc. are its qualities. Those Karma which develop and cultivate these Gunas are Brahmana's Karmas.

The mind in which Rajas Predominates and then comes Sattwa and Tamas is Kshatriya mind. This mind has Gunas like bravery, passion, expertancy in fighting, ruling power, attitude of doing for others etc. The Karmas which develop and make these qualities strong are Kshtriya's Karmas.

The third kind of mind has Rajas on the top, but with it there is no Sattwa but Tamas comes second and Sattwa is only in small degree. This combination is given the name of Vaishya. He seems more active but his actions are only for himself – no sense of doing for others or less sense of swaha. In 18th Adhyay, Bhagwan has shown his Karmas as farming and business and Gauraxa.

In case of Brahmana and Kshatriya Bhagwan has shown their Gunas but here in the case of Vaishya Bhagwan shows only Karma – not Gunas so we can say that in Kshatriya there must be some Qualities of Brahmana also though in a small amount. In the same way Vaishya also needs some of the qualities of Kshatriya. Then why is waishya given separate Varna? It is because his way of doing things is different. Vaishya is more self-centred and does not have much. Concern for doing for others.

The fourth kind of mind where Tamas Predominates Contains idleness, laziness, lethargic, way of performing work etc. This Varna is named as Shudra. Bhagwan says that its job is to serve the other three Varnas. The man with the Shudra mind lacks independent thinking or no capacity to initiate in any area on his own. He does that much work about which he is told and does only when it seems to him unavoidable or compulsory. He has no interest in working for even his own benefit. Shadra is also known as kimkar. It is a Sanskrit word used for one who goes on asking, "now what to do", "what to do" – (Kim Karomi) But the man with such a mind if develops the inner qualities of Vaishga, then from Shudra Varna he can move to the Varna of Vaishya and the same is true in the case of other varnas. Thus, in our Varna Vyavastha originally not based on birth and so movement among the varnas was also possible if one makes change in the combination of three Gunas of one's mind. Thus birth has no place in Vedic age in deciding Varnas. The Bhagwan has created this system on the basis of Guna and Karma.

The karma of all the different Varnas are quite different but no karma is considered either superior or inferior. Every work is equally important in its place. Though Guna Brahman (who can be anyone irrespective of his birth.

Generally Brahmin Varna has more respect as this varna has its roots into our Arsha Drashta Rishes – where on the top is Narayana and Sadashiv descending the Parampara to our Acharya. And so children born in this varna has special advantages as compared to other varnas.

But what happened with the change in time? Generally Brahman parents give birth of not only the

Brahman body but Brahman mind too. The child naturally needs a conducive atmosphere to maintain and develop the Brahman mind's Gunas. Mostly the child got such surroundings and remain in Brahman Varna. This process if continues for a long time and it did continue as our society was initially non-competing society. So he remains in the same varna as the son following his father's profession. Gradually a tradition is established in the society to decide varna in accordance to birth. And the whole varna vyavastha which was based on Guna and Karma became birth based. If one borns in Brahman family is considered as belong to Brahman Varna and so on.

Bhagwan says in the second line of the 13th Verse that I have created Chaturvarna on the basis of Guna and Karma but you know me as A-Karta/non-doer. In our Shastra we come across such contradictory statements and to understand that we need a teacher/acharya. What does Bhagwan want to convey here?

When we say that Brahman mind is more near to the desire for Moksha due to its specific qualities and they deserve respect as they have their roots in our Rishes, then one can ask then why Bhagwan gave me birth in Shudra or Vaishya Varna – Bhagwan did injustice to me. Here Bhagwan's answer is I do nothing. I am a non-doer…. You may have accumulated such Karmas in your innumerable past births that you were born to exhaust your Karmfal in the Shudra Varna. Your karma took you there. I am A-Karta. To make this non-dropship more clear we can cite one example of fire. Fire says I do not burn anything. I am a non-doer. You put your finger in fire and it burnt. Fire is as it is the nature of which is heat. You put your finger in fire and it is burnt. Fire has done nothing. Similarly according to your Karma in past janmas, you develop certain Vasanas and related other things which are responsible for your birth in certain varna, family, Socio-economic condition etc. Bhagwan is Akarta. On the other hand it is also true that the infinite being, all pervading, formless, changeless, immutable "Brahman" can neither be the doer, nor the creator. So it is the Bhagwan who is an avtar can say that I am the author of Charturvana, but the same Bhagwan in His own real Nature is non-doer.

The Varna Vyavastha invites much criticism specially from the young generation about the logic behind it. It should be always remembered that initially this system was based on Karma and Guna. Janma has nothing to do with that. Not only that but everyone has freedom to move from one varna to another by cultivating required qualities. And basically the whole system is geared to make one grow into Brahman (the Gunas of Brahman) which we may call Brahmantwa – that is near to Parmatman/Mox.

More over this four kinds of people who are described in our Shastra and Geeta as Brahman. Kshatriya, Vaishya and Shudra are visible all over the world. In every country we see different kinds of people having different mind-sets, though those names which we use are not used there. We see in the universe that some people have interest in study, research, innovating new things have certain qualities like skill of managing mind. Sense organs, have love for knowledge etc. Some have more proficiency in administration, management, fighting spirit for Dharma, maintaining law and order, protecting the nation from enemies etc. Still some others are interested in doing business, industrial endeavours, farming, etc. and remaining people have no interest in education, in knowing or leaving new things, no ambition, not that intelligence. They only do that much that is told to them. They are lazy and easy going people. They work as hands and legs of other three kinds of people. And we need such kind of people also to do certain jobs at the Lower Level of any organisation. But never forget that no job is inferior or superior. Every human being must be treated equally as human being by considering the dignity of labour.

In our own country as the value of money and economic consideration is given more importance, people began to do jobs which are not in accordance with their Varna and gradually not only it became based on birth but it gave rise to many other castes generated from every varna. And thus Hindu people became divided in so many different jaties. Politicians takes its advantage and still they are doing that. Hindus are totally ignorant about what was the original varna or jati Vyavastha was, Ved Vyas has described. Chaturvarna as the differentiation of the mental qualities and physical actions of the people. And it is made clear that not a man by birth or by any external physical mark or bodily action becomes a Brahman. Brahman he is by cultivating good Gunas, noble thoughts and other such Gunas like yam, niyam, swadhyay, sacred way of life etc. and these alone bring him Brahmantwa... Similarly Shudra is not one whose thoughts are tamasic but also he who likes a life of low endeavour for satisfying his animal like passions. So Varna was not at all birth based but it was according to the differentiations of Guna and Karma.

We are unfortunate that we forget what originally we are and we become divided into various jaties and politicians and those who have vested interest, take advantage and foolishly allow them to exploit us. Let me hope from the young generation to understand the Reality and bring back that system which enables us to grow from the level where we are to the level that is the goal of human life.

In Sanatan we are given four purusharth, Artha, Kama, Dharma and Moksha. Now Artha (to get basic necessities of life and security in everything) Karma (to get some comforts and to get those things that can give mental satisfaction), Dharma is also one of the Purusharth – not an end in itself – Dharma indicates good deeds, Karma done for others, for the benefit of the society. And the final goal of life is the fourth Purusharth and it is Moksh – a desire to be free from the cycle of birth and death.

Along with Purusharth four Ashrams are also given – Brahmcharyashram (period of time for study), Gruhsthashram (having a family and settling in life), Vanprasthashram (gradually leaving the household duties). At this stage the man gets time to think – who am I? What is Ishwar? Why am I here? And the last is Sanyas Ashram (where one leaves sansar and becomes Sanyasi and spends time in search of the Truth/Reality).

And last we have this Varna Vyavastha. According to Psychological differentiation of mind, people are classified in four Varnas – Brahman, Kshatriya, Vaishya and Shudra – depending on Guna and Karma. And among these four Varnas one can move from one Varna to another Varna by cultivating the corresponding Gunas.

What a beautiful system of processing the human mind from primary level to the highest possible height of inner growth and maturity!

The idea behind all these three systems is to motivate man work initially may be for his own interest but gradually in the process he learns to do for others, develop the sense of sacrifice/swaha, began to follow the way of Karmayogi while Passing through Grihasthashram, do his niyat karma, leaving aside his own likes and dislikes, offer it to the Ishwar, accepting Him as Karma fal Pradata and accept the result with balanced mind and thus, knowingly or unknowingly makes a change in the combination of these three Gunas of mind and can progress to Brahmanhood – develop the desire to be free from Sansar – Chakra/Moksha.

Thus, the whole system is so organised that it definitely takes man near to the goal of human birth which is considered very rare – if man enters into the system and lives his like as it is in the whole process at the end he will come out as an enlightened human being who is ready to receive the Atmagnan and get free.

But alas, most of the people do not even want to be free. They will enjoy this sansar though it frequently creates problems, sorrow, diseases, unhappiness in life – Even one has its own choice. What can be done otherwise?

But our Sanatan is very logical, has the right to ask a question which no other religion gives and says accept the things. Only Sanatan way of life says when by using your intellect and logic you can understand with the help of a teacher then only accept. And our Shastra will never disappoint you. There is everything you would like to have – Go deep into it and find out. You will get solution of any problem you face:

APPENDIX – 2

AVTAR – ITS PURPOSE
(PRAYOJAN)

In Sanatan we have the concept of Avtar – Where Ishwer assumes the body and comes on the earth. In Geeta Bhagwan says in the 7th verse of fourth chapter:

Yada Yada hi Dharmsya Glanirbhavati Bharata |
Abhyutthanamadhrmasya Tadatmanam
Srujamyaham | | (4-7)

Whenever there is a decay of righteousness, O, Bharat, and a rise of unrighteousness, then I manifest myself.

It is said here that "whenever there is decline of Dharma, I create for myself a body."

It is already made clear that the word, "DHARMA" is not used in the traditional sense to indicate a certain religion. But Dharma here means NIYAT KARMA – Duty – Doing the most appropriate Karma in the given situation is dharma. Only the human beings are given free will to select their Karma. In animals such freedom is not available. Only the man has the freedom to decide what action he will do or not to do or do it in some other way. And he is also free to misuse this freedom.

Dharmsya Glani means non performance of niyat karama aur Kartavya Karma. Now a man cannot remain without doing any karma even for a moment. And if he does not perform his duty/dharma, that means he is busy in doing unrighteous acts. Vedas say if you follow dharma, dharma will protect you. **Dharmo Raksati Raksitah.** if one does one's duty then there is no possibility of unrighteous karmas. But under the pressure of his Rag-Dwesh the man follows A-Dharma, does wrong and illegal activities.

The base of life is Dharma. And Generally people have respect for values like Satya, non-violence, love etc. Which are universal norms and which maintain harmony between individual and individual, individual and the family, individual and society etc. But all do not always go smoothly.. Sometimes an individual has to choose one – his own interests or the interest of family or society.

Here the individual is expected to choose which is the most appropriate in a given situation. His decision must be based on DHARM. But remember dharma is a relative term not absolute. Before exercising dharma one must think and apply one's Vivek – thus before deciding what to do – what is my dharma – comes two things – Vichar and Vivek – After applying these two, one can choose his right action.

Rashtrawad is a dharma – but if one's rashtrawad becomes dangerous for other nations as what happened in the case of Hitlar's rashtrawad then it remains no more a dharma. Similarly our Sanatan or Samanya dharma are our accepted values. But here also we should be careful and apply our thinking and Vivek before exercising them in practice. For example "Matrudevo Bhav, Pitrudevo Bhav" are Jeevan Mulyas. Shri Ramji and Bharat both know that. But Shri Ram accepted the wish of his father and went for vanvas, but Bharatji did not accept the wish of his mother and did not accept the position of the King. Here the value is the same but as per the situation the decision taken by both is different but most appropriate. Similarly, think about Shri Ram and Shri Krushna. The lives of both are value based. But before Ramji there is no Shakuni, no Duryodhan but Bhagwan Shri Krushna has to face all kinds of unrighteous people. So the way in which they interpret values is different.

To live a life based on Values is a cultured life while to live life under the hold of our raag-dwesh, our own self interest makes our life – just like an animal.

And when so-called leaders and politicians follow unrighteous activities, the whole society will be infected. The people who still try to follow value based life face various problems and harracement. The whole society lost its way and pious people pray to Ishwar to save them. And thus as the result of the Karma Prayers of good people–Ishwer manifests and assumes a human body.

Ishwar assumes a body and comes to the earth, whenever such a situation and vigorous people intensively pray to the Ishwer to save them. Now the question may arise in the mind of the youth – what is the purpose of prayojan of Avtar. Why does Ishwer have to assume a body?

Bhagwan says in the next verse.

**Paritranay Sadhunam Vinashay Cha Dushkruttam |
Dharmsansthapnarthay Sambhavami Yuge Yuge ||**

For the protection of good, for the destruction of the wicked and for the establishment of righteousness, I am born in every age.

Bhagwan says whenever there is decay in dharma I come to correct it – as per the situation demands as per the necessity of the state of affairs and as per the prayers made by righteous people. There is not any rule for that.

Then Bhagwan gives three purposes of His manifestation.

1. To protect Sadhus – Righteous persons.

2. To destroy wicked persons.

3. To establish dharma.

Bhagwan takes human body to protect Sadhu people. "Sadhu" does not always mean Sanyasi. Sadhu may or may not be Sanyasi but Sanyasi should be Sadhu. Sadhu is one who does his swadharm at any cost. He does have a sense of sacrifice for others. Performing dharm or duty always implies some sacrifice and that attitude takes one to the desire of Moksha. And on the other hand Sanyasi does not mean only saffron clothes, He is fully committed to Atmagnan. Dispassion and Tyag is implied in Sanyas which is not essential in Sadhu. Sadhu is one who does his Niyat Karm, never leaves his Swadharm and lives a righteous life.

Such Sadhu and Sanyasi people who want to live their life by performing their duty and always live in their Swadharm are required to be provided a conducive atmosphere in which they live their life smoothly.

To spread knowledge only Libraries and books are not enough, it needs Acharyas also who provide education and disciples who get this knowledge and for that they need free environment and protection where these people can do their work without any obstacles. By protecting such people only the dharma can be protected.

The people who are Sadhu, religious and having Shubh Vritty are to be appreciated by the society. Society must give them their due respect. Bhagwan reestablishes such practice in the society not only by providing confusive surroundings but also by giving them due respect and by appreciating their service too. Dharma can be protected only by protecting Dharmic people. Therefore the Primary purpose of Avtar is to protect Sadhu People.

The next purpose is to destroy the wickeds who always harrace and create obstacles in the way of righteous people. He will see that the people who have wicked mind sets should never be presented as an example before the society, never praised in public, but such elements are to be eliminated from the society at any cost. He creates such an atmosphere where what is good or value based is to be appreciated and what is wicked and Adharma based is to be destroyed.

Let us take the example for the young generation to understand this easily. If a student who comes daily to the college or university in his big and luxurious car and makes a show how rich he is and creates shor-sharaba in the campus moving like the hero. And if other students are impressed by him and appreciate his such behaviour and will try to follow and imitate him, that will spoil the whole atmosphere of the campus of the Institute.

So always appreciate and respect – what is good and criticise or avoid or destroy what causes harm to the society. Shri Ramji gives respect to Shabri, Shurbhan, Kevat, Vasishht, Bhardwaj as the Avtar is to protect and appreciate the Sadhu people. But at the same time He comes to destroy the wicked people.

Bhagwan may try to improve the mind-set of the wicked but if the inner wickedness is very strong then his destruction is necessary. Shri Ram has freed Marich by giving him due Punishment, when He saw that there is the possibility of being able to remove wickedness but kills Subahu. If any organ of the body becomes diseased and for saving the body if it is essential, to ampute that organ of the body it must be done. Similarly when a person or group of people cause great harm to the society or nation they must be eliminated for the benefit of mankind.

Thus, the very object of Avtar is to protect righteous people and to eliminate wicked people and establish Dharma. – Sanatan values which are universal.

We human beings are born as per our Karma accumulated in our innumerable past births. But the supreme reality which is the substratum for the whole pluralistic world when it assumes the body is not due to any Karma as Ishwer is non-doer/Akarta. His birth is divine and it takes place due to the prayers of righteous people to re-organise and reestablish DHARMA.

Without some equipment, electricity cannot, of its own accord, manifest itself. Similarly the Supreme Cannot project out into a Divine or as a mortal ego, unless there is some desires to Precipitate the manifestation – So He comes as the result of the Karma of Prayers done very intensively by His devotees to protect the good people, destroy the bad and reestablish the Dharma.

As we create our dream world with its different objects – Jad and Chetan – like trees, roads, rivers, buildings, cars, mountains, people, our friends and what not? Even we create our own bodies too. There to create all these we do not need any raw material. It manifests by mere Sankalpa of our mind. It is only a projection of our mind. In fact, I myself become my dream world – There is no difference between me and my dream world. Similarly the Ishwer manifests Himself as this world including the bodies of all of us that I see front of me. And as I create my own body in my dream world, Ishwer also assumes one body for Himself if need arises, if prayers are made for His help in its creation (world that we see) he creates a body for himself And we call it Avtar.

Ved Vyas presents Shri Krushna as Avtar in Mahabharat and here we hear it from the mouth of Bhagwan Himself in Bhagavad Geeta. So this is the concept of "Avtar " in our way of Sanathan life.

www.ingramcontent.com/pod-product-compliance
Lightning Source LLC
Chambersburg PA
CBHW020323180726
47991CB00018B/370